LUMINOUS HEALING

Other books by Peter Bowes:

ॐ

Traveler

Spiritual Astrology I & II

Luminous Healing

Peter Bowes

Sophia Publishing
Woodstock, IL

Luminous Healing

First Edition

Printed in the United States of America by Lulu

ISBN 978-0-359-11792-5

SophiaPublishing.com
Woodstock, IL 60098

Cover Art: Ljiljana Mlinarevic

CONTENTS

SCIENCE OF LIGHT

Light

God is Light - and while this is by no means an adequate definition of Divine Being, it is true that the infinitude of Light approaches about as near as the finite mind of man can hope to come in an understanding of His Nature.

The sun of our solar system is the brightest light which is evident to our sense of vision, and of course it is also much more than that, acting as the very sustainer of all life on earth. For this reason it was often worshiped by the ancients, its radiance appearing as a perfect symbol for the mediator who functions between natural man and the great Invisible Light and Being of God.

The sun is sometimes called the great Healing Benefactor, assisting generously in the restoration of health to those who have gotten off balance. Persons with most types of illness are encouraged to spend some time in the sunshine each day, making sure to exercise moderation and good judgment, to measure the time spent, for one must avoid overexposure to its powerful rays. We have all experienced the joyous lift in our spirits that comes from morning sunshine, another important factor in healing, and in arousing the desire to get better.

Waves

Light is one of many different kinds of electromagnetic radiation in the part of the spectrum which includes infrared, visible light, ultraviolet and x-rays. These light rays all travel at the same rate of speed (in a vacuum), this speed being measured at close to 186,282 miles.

All radiations emitted from a luminous body move through space in a perfect rhythmic vibration. Light is a form of energy traveling through the universe in waves like those on a body of water. While not directly visible as the crests and troughs of waves on water, their presence can be demonstrated by indirect methods. The distance between the topmost point of one wave crest, and that of the crest next to it, is called one wavelength. Although the speed of travel is the same for various types of light, the distance between the wave crests determines the vibratory rate, called frequency, or number of vibrations per second at which they oscillate. Those with higher frequency have more wave crests per unit of measurement, are spaced closer together, and these are vibrating faster, though their beams or rays reach the goal simultaneously with the slower longer waves which are spaced farther away.

Some idea of vibrations can be illustrated by a long-stretched string. If it is struck at one end, a hump will form and it will travel the full length of the string, but the form itself is displaced. In water waves, the quantity remains but the form is displaced. With light in free space, the form is unchanged but any object or refractive medium interrupts this simplicity of form.

Any wave is a vibrating motion that travels along. In sound waves this vibration is forward and backward as the waves go on, but in light waves it is from side to side. Nothing really quivers or wiggles as light moves along. Instead, the waves are made up of electrical and magnetic forces that get stronger and weaker at regular intervals. The important thing is that these forces are crosswise to the way the waves are traveling.

Light waves are about 1/50,000 of an inch in length. At the other end of the scale, some waves of radio are more than a mile in length. There is quite a difference between the nature of water and light waves. Light waves are similar to radio waves. Both are called "electromagnetic radiation" but they differ in the rate at which their waves vibrate, that is their frequency. Light waves vibrate faster and are shorter.

That there are other rays in sunlight besides the colored light that we see in the spectrum can be proved with the help of photographic film and a thermometer. If photographic film is held just outside a spectrum of sunlight at the violet end, it becomes exposed as if light were falling on it. This shows that there are invisible electromagnetic rays there that we call ultraviolet rays because they are beyond the violet end of the spectrum. If a thermometer is held on the other side of the spectrum, just past the red end, the mercury begins to rise. This shows that there are invisible rays there that are warming the bulb of the thermometer. Though it is ultraviolet rays in sunlight that cause sunburn, the infrared rays make much of the heat you feel when sunlight falls on your skin.

Corpuscles

The corpuscles of light are like tiny particles of packaged energy, and are called photons. The different colors of light are explained as having photons of different energy – those of blue light possessing twice the amount of energy as those of red. The energy of the photons is directly proportional to the frequency of the light-waves. For example, while x-rays have a wave-like character, their higher frequency gives the particles great penetrating power, allowing them to be used for taking pictures through matter that is opaque to visible light. Light has a dual nature represented equally well by waves or photons. The two are merely complementary aspects of the same reality. Both light and matter may behave either as waves or photons. The light arising from an atom has a spherical wave form.

Scattered Light

When light strikes an atom, it causes electrons to re-emit light. The quality of this scattered light will depend upon the nature of the atoms, as well as on the source of light. The compounding effect of a number of atoms produces a mixture of light reaction as it strikes the atoms. The most primitive example of scattering is the light in the sky, where light from the sun will have scattered through a broad path of atoms between itself and the observer, the atoms unsystematic and irregular in placement. In working with crystals, whose atoms are in orderly position, the light is focused according to specified intentions.

Beams and Rays

A narrow path of light is usually called a beam of light. A flashlight or a searchlight throws a beam. If the beam is made much narrower, it amounts to a ray or laser. To show how light moves from one place to another, one might draw a bundle of rays of light, which could be thought of as tiny arrows moving through space. This bundle again would be called a beam of light. They are electromagnetic forces traveling along together at enormous speed.

In one short second, light travels fast enough to more than circle the globe seven times. When light goes through a transparent substance, such as glass or water, it is slowed down. It can travel only about two-thirds as fast through a piece of glass as it can through empty space or air, and about three-quarters as fast through water as through air. This slowing down is important, as it makes it possible for us to bend beams of light, and thus to make prisms, lenses, eye-glasses, telescopes, microscopes, cameras and other devices that help us to see better.

Reflection

When light strikes a reflective medium, such as a mirror, a pool of water, or any other surface, the ray will bounce off in the opposite direction at exactly the same degree of angle as that from which it came.

Refraction

When a light ray moves from one substance to another so that its speed is changed, the ray changes direction. This is called refraction.

There are some objects that do not reflect light, but permit it to pass through, while slowing it down somewhat according to the density of the object. Water, which is denser than air, will slow the light velocity by about one-fourth, while glass will slow its speed of travel by one third. One can observe the changed effect in water, by dangling an object partially below and partially above the water's surface.

Light directed head on at glass will not deflect or bend the ray of light, it will pass straight through. In order for refraction to occur, light must strike the medium at an angle other than ninety degrees. Thus the spectrum colors reach the edge of the surface in different time sequence, so they are "surprised" into manifesting one by one in the rainbow colors of the spectrum.

SUNLIGHT AND CLIMATE

In olden days, the wise mothers used to massage their children with pure cow's melted butter called "ghee" and used to expose them to the morning sun. In temperate zones there is more latitude in the time of day when the skin may be exposed, but even so, around ten o'clock in the morning is usually quite fine and safer for small children.

Sunlight is the simplest and most natural way to insure vitamin D in the body and this vitamin is necessary to the utilization of calcium in the system. Therefore, sunlight, along with foods which are adequate in calcium content, helps insure proper bone growth and good teeth. Sunlight can physically be absorbed by the unbroken skin.

In sunbathing, one should expose the skin only a few minutes the first day, slowly increasing the amount of time each day, until an hour at most can be safely enjoyed. Sunshine includes not only the visible portion of radiation from the sun, but also the invisible, such as ultraviolet and infrared rays.

Ultraviolet

Ultraviolet light can cause sunburn. At the beach on a hazy day, when the sun does not appear to be very bright, a person can get a particularly bad sunburn because so much ultraviolet light is scattered in all directions by the tiny water droplets in the air. Fortunately, the earth's atmosphere absorbs the short ultraviolet waves more strongly than it does those waves we see with, so protects us somewhat from them.

The higher one goes up in the atmosphere, the more likely he is to be sunburned. At even five or six miles up in the air, the risk of sunburn and damage to the eyes is very great. Because ultraviolet waves do not go through ordinary glass, however, goggles and window panes give good protection.

The invisible ultraviolet radiation that causes tanning, comprises only a very small portion of the total radiation. Nevertheless, it is very important to health, producing vitamin D by its action on substances in the skin and in plants. Ultraviolet waves are important because they kill bacteria. Dishes and drinking glasses can be sterilized by proper exposure to strong ultraviolet rays. But while it is an important germicidal agent, the contaminated atmosphere over large cities robs radiation of practically all the shorter wavelengths.

Radiation from the sun is the ultimate source of nearly all energy that is essential for the maintenance of plant and animal life on the earth, and the operation of more natural phenomena on the surface of the earth. It is the electromagnetic energy in sunlight that warms the earth. When the light hits the earth, part of it changes to heat. If the steady stream of sunlight ever stopped, the temperature of the earth would drop to around 450 degrees below zero. Then nothing could live here. Visible radiation is commonly termed light; however the word "light" now has a broader meaning and includes the ultraviolet or that invisible portion immediately adjoining the shortest wavelength of visible radiation. The visible portion comprises nearly one-half of the total radiation from the sun which is actually received at the surface of the earth, and the infrared radiation, chiefly known for its heat-producing characteristics, accounts for almost all of the other half.

An excess of radiation, due to factors such as atomic explosions which rupture the earth's outer layer of ozone, are thought to be responsible for some skin cancer. However, in traveling through to reach earth's surface, this radiation is absorbed and weakened by various constituents of the atmosphere. It is also scattered by air molecules and this scattering occurs in the short wavelengths, giving the sky its blue color as seen from the surface of the earth. To an observer in the stratosphere with fewer air molecules above him, the sky appears dark.

Why do clouds look white? A cloud floating in the air is made up of many small drops of water. Each drop has a curved surface, so it scatters the sunlight that strikes it, scattering all colors in the sunlight equally. So when our eyes receive this light with all the colors mixed in it, as they are in sunlight itself, we see the cloud as something white. When larger particles or droplets of water in the form of mist or fog are suspended in the atmosphere, the visibility is much reduced, and thus results in a loss of the blue color in the sky.

On a clear day, the atmosphere consists of air molecules, dust particles and water droplets, most if them small in size compared to the wavelength of visible light. The sky appears blue to us because although sunlight passes freely through the ordinary thickness of atmospheric gases, these small particles scatter part of the light. Violet light, whose wavelength is much shorter, is scattered about nine times more effectively than the longer red waves. Therefore the blue range becomes more visible.

At sunrise or sunset, the angle of the sunlight has less effect on the short wavelengths, as the sun's rays travel a long path through the turbid lower atmosphere. There is less scattering of the blue and violet rays, thus causing colors to appear from the longer wavelengths of the red and yellow range.

Northern Lights

Sometimes on dark nights, colored lights can be seen dancing in the northern sky, stretching in big streamers or fan shapes all the way from overhead down to the northern horizon. These lights, also called aurora borealis, occur when streams of electrons from the sun strike the atoms in the upper part of the earth's atmosphere. The reason these lights in the sky are brightest near the north and south poles is that the earth is a giant magnet. Its magnetic forces send electrons from the sun spiraling in paths around the magnetic poles, and these produce the light when they strike atoms in the rarefied air.

Climate

The prime cause of weather and climate is the amount of the solar radiation intercepted by the earth. The angle of the sun's rays to the horizontal plane of the earth is an important factor, as seen by the differences in climate between summer and winter, and between the poles and the equator. The rays come in with more of a slant in winter because that hemisphere of the earth is then tipped away from the sun. As a result, the same amount of energy is spread over a larger surface in winter and there is less heating.

Man changes gradually to cope with the environment in which he finds himself. For example, in very high altitudes one finds persons of larger lung capacity and higher concentration of blood corpuscles than at low altitudes.

There are essentially three skin types found in human beings.

1. The pinkish-white, which burns when exposed in certain short wavelengths in the solar and sky radiation. It is found in the descendants of tribes from northwestern Europe, where sunshine is rare.

2. The second type is chocolate-brown or black, which is completely unaffected by solar radiation. Presumably this pigmentation was originally acquired at the tropical margins of the deserts, and in the savannas.

3. The third skin type is changeable, taking different shades in the individuals, variously described as creamy white, olive, yellow, red or brown. The primary distinction is that it can

pale when covered, and darken or tan when exposed to the sun, an adaptation to the widespread climatic type where seasons alternate between cloudy rain periods and bright sky.

Individuals tend to be bigger in cold climates, and smaller in the warmer parts of the earth. Metabolism rates are higher in the cold climates than in the hot. This is due to the fact that heat produced by metabolism is normally lost through the skin, but where the temperature exceeds eighty-three degrees and perspiration starts, cooling by evaporation takes place. At high temperatures and low humidity man loses large quantities of water. There is wisdom in avoiding exertion at midday and better to work mornings and evenings, and take a long midday siesta.

One need not be a scientist to observe the effect of sunlight on growing things. Anyone having house plants can notice how spindly and pale most plants become after time away from direct light. They begin to bend toward the nearest window, reaching to catch sunlight needed to convert substances, which have been drawn from the roots up to the leaves, into usable food energy. The growth of seedlings indoors can be promoted and sped up by use of artificial light where natural sunlight is insufficient. Photosynthesis is the process by which green plants harness the energy of sunlight, as absorbed by chlorophyll, to build organic compounds from carbon dioxide, inorganic salts and water. "Photosynthesis" literally means "putting together with light."

SOUND IN RELATION TO LIGHT

Sound has a place alongside the science of light, due to many of the same characteristics such as wavelength, reflection, refraction, scattering and diffraction. But light is a finer and faster vibrating form of energy. The science relating to sound is called acoustics. Philosophers and mystics believed that there was a definite correlation between the color spectrum and that of sound, that sound vibration touched upon one's inner color consciousness and that colors aroused an inner attunement akin to music.

Two systems were developed to match the octave of the musical keyboard to the color spectrum. They agreed on red, orange and yellow as corresponding to musical notes C, D and E respectively. But at F they diverged as follows:

1. F, green yellow; G, green; A, blue; B, violet
2. F, green; G, blue; A, indigo; and B, violet

Science has described a scale of vibrations beginning with two per second. When the number of pulsations per second is repeatedly doubled, a series of octaves results. Sound has a lower rate of pulsation than light.

The key of C, called "Middle C" in the musical scale, occurs at 256 vibrations per second. This produces a corresponding effect on the human ear to that of the note. As one can move up the musical scale, in a similar way one can move up the rate of vibrations by forty doublings of the vibration of Middle C, and arrive at the vibration that produces the speed required for the appearance of the color red. For at this finer point, the vibrations are produced to which your sight center responds, receiving the sensations of "red."

At the fifteenth octave of measurement, these waves of vibration become inaudible to the human ear. The octaves from twentieth to thirty-fifth are those of electricity. The thirty-sixth to forty-fifth, are nerve currents in the body. Forty-sixth through forty-eighth are octaves of heat vibrations. Following there are several octaves of light, of which visible light and the whole range of the color spectrum cover only one octave. (The audible sound range by comparison comprises some nine or ten octaves.) Beyond visible light are five octaves of ultraviolet light, ten octaves of x-rays and so on.

A person emits sound stimuli when he speaks; the listener experiences sound through hearing. The result of the processes of speech is some motion of the air in front of the mouth, and a person hears because there is some motion of the air at the entrance of the ear. Sound is the result of motion in some medium. The human voice operates by forcing air from the trachea to vibrate the vocal cords. This in turn sets into vibration the air in the cavities of the throat and mouth, and the resulting disturbance emerges from the lips.

Light waves are very much shorter than either water waves or sound waves. Sound waves traveling through the air do not have humps and hollows, as water waves do. Instead there are places where air is slightly squeezed together. In between, the air is slightly thinned out. The sound is carried by a set of these pushes and pulls, moving along through the air.

The velocity of sound waves in air increases with temperature; at room temperature it is roughly 767 miles per hour. This is very much slower than the speed of light. Therefore the sound of a crash of thunder is heard after the lightning flash is seen. You can measure the distance of a flash of lightning from here you are standing by counting the number of seconds between seeing it and hearing it. The delay will be about five seconds per mile from the flash to you.

Sound waves, like those of light, are reflected when they strike an appropriate surface. An echo illustrates this. Sound bounces off the face of a cliff, for example, and returns toward the direction from which it came. Speaking in a closed room is easier than in an open space, due to the gentle reflection of sound from the walls and other surfaces, all blending simultaneously. If reflection is too exaggerated due to hard or metallic surfaces, the echoes may become noticeable, then certain sound-absorbing materials such as cork, fabric, or perforated materials should be introduced to absorb some of the sound.

Sound waves travel faster in warm air than in cold. This causes a sound mirage, in that the sound will reach the ears as though it came from a different direction. Sound traveling with the wind moves more easily than against it. An object waved back and forth with less frequency than fifteen cycles per second would not be audible. An object moving any faster than that should become audible if the intensity is sufficient and it will remain audible up to a movement of 20,000 cycles per second. The higher frequency sounds are called ultrasonic waves. Ultrasonic waves tend to travel in beams like light, whereas slow frequency audible sound waves tend to spread in every direction from the source, radiating outward like ripples on a pond into which a stone has been dropped.

The power in speech sound waves varies, being much larger for vowels than for consonants. Hearing with two ears rather than one leads to the ability to detect the direction of sound waves. Sound waves set the eardrum into vibration, and this motion is communicated via the body ossicles (a kind of solid acoustic filter) to the oval window of the cochlea, a spiral cavity. The flexible basilar membrane in the cochlea can vibrate under the impact of motions of the cochlear fluid. Fine hairs in the adjacent organ of corti in the cochlea communicate these vibrations to terminals of the auditory nerve. The human ear is a vulnerable receiver, highly attuned, and deserves a harmonious sound environment.

"Music hath charms to soothe the savage beast," and listening to the various types can easily induce different moods or emotions. Music thus has therapeutic value in treating those with emotional disturbance, or inspiring interest in those who have lapsed into apathy. Light classical symphonic music gives the best results generally. It helps restore inner harmony to one who has gotten off balance. For the listless person who needs cheering, something a bit livelier would help. Avoid the hard beat of rock music as it has a shattering and disruptive effect on the nervous system, reducing persons to a jittery and unstable condition and upsetting the harmonies of nature. It can tear down the spiritual work and growth you are attempting to accomplish.

Animals respond readily to light classical music, when gently played. Even goldfish seem to enjoy it. In poultry houses or dairy barns, the output of eggs and milk can be increased with the use of music. It has been found that carefully selected music, played with taste, not too loud or inconsistently, aids employees in industry to maintain a better outlook and grow less tired with their work.

The Egyptian hierophant taught that the universe is called forth from chaos by ordered rhythmic sound. In the beginning of any cycle of manifestation it is the sound vibrations which come into expression before the more rapid pulsations of light. Hindus say "Through sound the world stands." They classify sound has having two types, the unlettered and the lettered. The former is that which could be caused by striking two objects together. The latter is articulated sound, words and sentences, and conveys intelligence. Such sound is said to be eternal. They place sound as the first of the gunas, or principles, out of which emanated the second principle, that of touch.

The secret of mantras has been carefully guarded by the mystics, because "Out of sound every form comes, and in sound every form lives." They teach that sound is the quality of the Akasha. It is the all-pervading fifth essence, having the characteristic quality of pure space. Out of all things come, and into it, all return.

Changing the mood of the music from sadness to joy, or from vigorous to peaceful has a distinct effect on the feelings of the listener. Each ganglion of the sympathetic nervous system is in harmony with a particular musical note, and responds to that note. Each musical note in turn corresponds with a certain color hue. Some musical sounds and some colors "jangle" the nerves, while others produce a pleasant or a beneficial reaction.

COLORS IN NATURE

"You couldn't live on this earth unless you had some of every one of its elements in you."
-   Father Paul

Natural color has more to do with one's well being than is often realized. The blue of space, the sky, is restful. The green of foliage is more enlivening than the browns of autumn; therefore green may be said to have a tonic effect and brown an earth-like effect. The blue of the sky with the brown in autumn give to the system the poignant effect of violet. The red of sunrise and sunset has a different effect upon the organism than the red reflected from the earth, the former being stimulating, the latter irritating.

The vast diversity of color in nature, and in living forms, is a subject of universal wonderment, a delight to the eye. In agriculture, the farmer quickly recognizes the stages of growth and ripening of his crops by observing the changing color pigmentation as they mature. In the diagnosis and treatment of disease, the physician is often aided by visible signs and symptoms concerning the state of health, as reflected by the colors of tissues and body fluids.

Precious Stones

Precious stones, such as diamonds, flash colored light that is very beautiful. These transparent stones are formed of materials that slow down light waves very markedly. In a pure diamond, light travels scarcely half as fast as it does in air. Light that shines into such a cut stone is refracted in many directions. The "fire" of a good diamond comes from the breaking up of white light into many colors by its tiny prisms. The greater the index of reflection, the greater the extent to which a light beam is deflected upon entering to leaving that medium. Diamonds owe their brilliance to that very high index of refraction.

Phosphorescent Light

You have seen luminous materials that glow in the dark. These materials are either phosphorescent or radioactive. A phosphorescent material must first be exposed to light before it will glow. Some mineral substances have this property, especially phosphorus, from a Greek word meaning "light bringing."

A piece of phosphorus glows in the dark as its atoms combine with the oxygen in the air. A firefly can emit quite a bright light by producing on the surface of its abdomen two chemicals whose molecules combine and emit cold light. In fact, one of the coolest lights known is that produced by a firefly. This is ninety percent light and only ten percent heat.

Black light

If a tube is surrounded by a special glass that absorbs visible light, only the ultraviolet light comes through. This is what we call black light. Ultraviolet rays and black light are also used to sterilize milk and to keep meat stored in a refrigerator from spoiling. Black light can be used to detect fingerprints not visible to the human eye in ordinary visible light. If the prints are treated with a florescent powder and exposed to black or florescent light they will show up clearly.

Stars

A star, and our sun is one of them, is a self-luminous object that shines by radiation derived from energy sources within itself. By contrast, planets shine by reflected light only, while gaseous and diffuse nebulae may shine either by reflected light or by fluorescence.

The distance of stars from the earth is measured in terms of light years, a unit of interstellar space measurement equal to the distance traversed by light in one year – that is, approximately six trillion miles. Probably the largest amount of information that is attainable for any star is obtained from its spectrum. From this can be determined some idea of the brightness and property of distant stars. Even with the naked eye one can observe certain differences in color. While most stars appear blue-white, Betelgeuse in Orion, for example is deep red, and Albireo in Cygnus consists of two stars – one blue and the other orange.

Melanin

If an apple is cut so that its flesh is exposed to the air, the surface of the cut begins to turn brown. The brown color is caused by a pigment called melanin that is formed by the action of the air on one of the chemicals that is in the apple. Melanin is also found in the skin and human hair. Because of the high frequency, each photon of ultraviolet light has a high amount of energy. It can damage the cells in a living body. So the body needs protection against ultraviolet rays. The melanin in our skins gives us this protection by absorbing the ultraviolet rays before they can do any harm.

Dark colors evidence the presence of the melanin pigment - dark feathers, hair or eyes. Certain albino animals fail to develop melanin in their tissues. Urochrome, the principle yellow pigment of urine, is considered to be a modified melanin. In certain diseases melanin precursors cause urine to darken as oxidation occurs on standing.

The dark hairs of mammals contain a higher trace of copper than do pale hairs. If the intake of copper falls well below the minimal requirement of a fraction of a milligram per day, the new hairs which emerge are less dark. Spherical microgranules of melanin are randomly distributed within the dried cortical cells of all colors of hair, imparting varying degrees of hue from light to dark, depending on the presence of micro granules of melanin. Human red hair, unlike any other hair from humans or animal, is unique in its iron-rich pigment. Red poultry feathers yield a similar substance.

All human skin, except albinos, contains greater or lesser amounts of melanin. In fair-skinned races the corium, or deeply lying skin layer, contains but little of the pigment. But darker races carry heavier dermal deposits, fortified by numbers of smaller melanocytes in the upper skin layer, or epidermis. Exposure to sunlight causes tanning with a gradual increase of melanin pigment, which in turn helps protect underlying tissues from injurious sunrays.

Certain fish placed in black-lines containers have been found to increase the melanophores of the skin, which after transfer to pale containers, they gradually lose it again. Another interesting phenomena has been observed among the fishes of rapid darkening of the skin through melanization. The Tasmanian whitebait, as it approaches sexual ripeness, develops an increasing number of melanophores, then after spawning shows extensive darkened areas of the skin.

Indigo occurs in many plants, and has long been useful as a blue dye. It does not occur in the tissue of healthy animals, but certain chemical derivatives of it are found in secretory and excretory products. Tyrian Violet is a product secreted by several species of snail, of the genera murex and purpura.

Lyochrome

Lyochromes, flavins, are synthesized by bacteria, yeasts and green plants. A very important one of these, called riboflavin, is identical with Vitamin B_2. This is not manufactured by animals, but must be derived from plant sources. It is part of an enzyme capable of combining with molecular oxygen, thus developing a yellow color.

A nutritional lack of riboflavin in the diet retards growth, causes development of cataracts, and impairment of cellular respiration. The compound is not stored in quantity. Milk, eggs, liver, kidney, blood and muscles contain riboflavin.

Most pigments have roles related to their light-absorbing or light-reflecting qualities. In the eyes of some creatures, certain pigments in the violet range regulate the admission of light. In others, reflecting pigments cause the night eye shine.

It is possible that light-absorbing and reflecting pigments in the skin may be involved in a primitive mechanism for temperature regulation in certain cold-blooded species, for example the desert horned toad. In the cool of the morning its skin is dark, and absorbs heat rays; as the temperature rises during the day its skin blanches, thereby reflecting heat rays away from the body.

White in the animal kingdom is sometimes due to special white substances deposited in the tissues; in other cases it is due to the lack of colored substances – their place being taken by air. In the hair of white mammals and the plumage of white birds, this may be of value in retarding heat radiation. It appears that these are given to them for protective coloration; certain smaller arctic animals change their white winter coat for darker fur during the summer. There are many animals who can change their shade, or even their actual color, slowly or almost instantaneously, to conform to their background and camouflage their whereabouts.

Male birds are usually more brilliant of plumage than the female. This is for the protection of the female during the nesting period when she must melt into the background, unobserved, sitting on the nest until the babies have hatched and are safely launched.

Plant colors are predominantly green due to the prevalence of green chlorophyll in the leaves and stems of most plants, grasses and trees. Chlorophyll, one of the most important pigments in nature, is capable of channeling the radiant energy of sunlight into chemical energy usable in the reactions of the cell through the process called photosynthesis. Chemically it is related to hemoglobin, the "heme" in the red blood pigment, as well as to the respiratory enzymes called cytochromes. Chlorophyll absorbs nearly all of the red light that falls on it. Plants use the energy of the absorbed light to build sugar molecules out of water and carbon dioxide. The light reflected by the chlorophyll in leaves is that which is left over after the red light has been absorbed. This kind of light mixture imparts to growing plants their green appearance.

Carotene

In the plant world, the carotenoids are almost universally present in the yellow to orange-red colorants of nature, such as in carrots or marigolds. Carotene is the raw material from which vitamin A is made. It is changed into vitamin A by the action of ultraviolet rays.

When the leaves change color from green to different shades of yellow and red, this is the result of the carotene in the leaves. Carotenoids are a group of red, orange, or yellow pigments. These are present in many plants and creatures, concentrated particularly in the yolks of eggs, sexual organs, hair, skin, eyes and milk. Marine animals derive carotenoids from rich supplies of seaweed or microscopic underwater plants. In man, the skin may turn slightly yellow from an excessive intake of such carotene-rich foods as carrots or oranges. This otherwise harmless condition is called artificial jaundice, and clears up when intake is reduced. The bright color of the flamingo, as well as many fishes and other creatures, is due to some derivatives of carotenoid present in their systems.

Flavonoids

The flavonoids impart yellow color to certain flowers and are found in some insects. These are nitrogenous, water-soluble pigments called porphyrins. They are found in plant chlorophyll, and in animal hemoglobin, present in the red blood cells of most creatures. Hemoglobin is responsible for the pink to red color of the combs and wattles of birds, and the skin of man. Certain underwater creatures fade in aerated water, but increase in redness when placed in water with a poor supply of oxygen, apparently a physiological adaptation toward survival. Hemoglobin is also present in the bacteria-harboring root of peas, beans and other legumes. It is believed to serve as a catalyst for the chemical fixation of atmospheric nitrogen in the soil, a well known property of the root nodules of legumes.

The autumn coloring of leaves is due to the disappearance of chlorophyll, as it decomposes at the approach of winter, and the formation of anthocyanins. Anthocyanin gives both violet-red color to autumn leaves, and the red-violet appearance to young new growth. Certain mineral deficiency of plants can be detected by the formation of red anthocyanin coloration. The flavonoids include anthocyanin, responsible for the red, blue, mauve, and violet colors; and the anthoxanthins, ranging from colorless to yellow. The latter is responsible for white, cream or ivory.

BASICS OF COLOR

The Color Spectrum

Mastering the spectrum is the preliminary discipline of all who seek to make themselves prisms of Light. The test comes when the Divine ego or will takes over, for the Power can be used for good or evil. The spectrum in proper proportions produces light. The positive side of any force lies in the fine rather than the coarse principles, in the intangible rather than the material side of things. The pure white light of the sun is best for ordinary use especially for well persons but under certain conditions various colors are more effective.

Color therapy is based on eternal truth. Human beings occupy the highest level of refinement in the visible world. They animate not only the physical being but the mental and feeling side of our nature as well, thus beneficially affecting our whole self. The exquisite and soft character of a force is an indication of its power, not its weakness.

Chroma from the Greek, means color. Colors are classified by achromatic and chromatic colors. The achromatic include black, white and the intermediate grays, varying only in brilliance. The chromatic colors vary also in hue and saturation.

There are seven major colors of the visible spectrum. These relate to the seven planes of manifestation, the seven major planets, the seven glandular centers in the body and the seven great cosmic periods. These have a significant relationship to the seven major chakras in the body. Each sympathetic ganglion corresponds to a particular musical note and each musical note corresponds to a particular color of the spectrum. Different wavelengths of vibration are not colors or sounds, but they excite our sensations of color at the receptor sights (senses) which can pick up that set of vibrations easily. Sight is the range of perception. Our eyes are able to receive and we interpret these sensations inside our brains as colors. Higher colors control the lower, linking together all planes.

The seven major colors are Red, Orange, Yellow, Green, Blue, Indigo and Violet. These are separated into primary and secondary colors. The primary colors are Red, Yellow and Blue. These colors tell of the resurrection of the Light of Spirit from the physical through discipline. The action and reaction of the primary and secondary colors involves the Self and evolves the Universe.

The secondary colors are Orange, Green, and Violet. The secondary colors constitute the lines between the planes and tell of the descent of the Light of Spirit to the physical through application. Secondary colors are produced by a combination of two primary colors: Red + Yellow = Orange, Yellow + Blue = Green, Red + Blue = Violet.

Tertiary colors are produced by combining two secondary colors. Green + Violet = slate; Green + Orange = citrine; Orange + Violet = Russet. Colors are very indefinite in most people's minds for many have never looked at the spectrum either through a prism or a spectroscope and have never compared them with the reds and blues seen in pigments and dyes. The dull navy blue color generally called indigo, for instance, is very different from the beautiful deep spectrum indigo.

The Eye

Visual judgments of color tell only the predominant behavior at the surface of any opaque object. In fact, appearances of all kinds are relatively misleading. To the eye, ordinary matter appears to be continuous, presenting an unbroken surface but science tells us it is not. If we had ultramicroscopic vision we might see through many things that now appear quite solid, and the smooth tops of tables would be made of mountains and valleys.

If the eye could see in the ultraviolet region of the spectrum, substances that emit ultraviolet would appear to be surrounded by an aura or halo. Human bodies would be seen surrounded by some sort of penumbra, visible to clairvoyants.

The eye is an image-catching device. The process of vision in all creatures begins with light entering the eye and bringing with it the information it has picked up in touching or passing through the objects in its path. These light patterns travel through the various parts of the eye until just the image is cast upon the retina of the eye, just as the picture is thrown upon film by the camera. It is the work of the iris, the colored part of the eye, to control the amount of light that enters by contracting or stretching as needed, to shrink or enlarge the pupil.

There are two kinds of light sensitive neurons in the retina, the rods and the cones. The cones are sensitive to colors, and the rods only to white light. The rods and cones are the real light receptors. Impulses resulting from the stimulation of the rods and cones by light travel into dendrites in the optic nerve, and then to sight centers in the cerebrum and occipital lobe. The rods do not function well unless plenty of vitamin A is present in the retina.

When we see the color of an object, it is the last step in a chain of events that begins at a light source. The light source generally sends out a mixture of light rays of many wavelengths. As the rays pass through the air to the object, the air attenuates some of the light of short wavelengths by scattering it. When the light falls on the object, the object removes some more light by absorbing it. What is left of the light is then reflected or transmitted from the object through the air to our eyes. Once again the air removes some light. The color we see depends on the kind of light mixture that finally reaches our eyes. But it depends, too, on the nature of our eyes, and the message that our eyes send to the brain.

The world is colorless to some people who are called colorblind. Their optical nerves do not react to color. It is generally accepted that the world was colorless to prehistoric man who was color-blind. The faculty to see color has developed slowly over the ages. Color blindness is the inability to distinguish between certain colors. Genuine color blindness, or complete inability to see colors, is quite rare, affecting only one person in 300,000.

Color Hues

Hue is the difference in the color itself and this depends on the wavelength of light; this is what we see as colors. Brightness is the luminosity of the same colors within each hue. Chroma is the purity of the color; truly pure is free of gray. Saturation is the purity, quality of cleanness or brilliance as opposed to drab or dirty. Monochromatic mixtures give the purest saturation. Tint combines a color with white producing a variation in brightness. Shade combines a color with black to produce a variation of saturation or purity. Tone combines a color with gray, which is a mixture of black and white. By mixing a color with its complement, we can also darken it without changing its hue.

Unless you pass light through a prism and spread it out, you cannot tell exactly what colors, or wavelengths are in it. Something that appears red to the eye may prove to have some orange, yellow or red in its spectrum. Color wheels show the relationship between the various colors. The hues are arranged in the same order as they come out of a prism, that is, according to wavelength. The one exception to this arrangement is indigo and violet, which do not actually appear in the spectrum because they are a mixture of red and blue rays. However, to form the completed circle, they are arranged in the proper order between the blue and red. Between the visible violet and the visible red are indigo, blue, green, yellow and orange. There are an infinite number of colors that we cannot perceive. The infrared and ultraviolet rays are invisible to the eye but can be demonstrated by various instruments.

The hues red, blue and green have a very important property. If we mix the right amount of light of these three hues, we can match closely any hue on the color circle. For this reason, red, blue and green are often called primary colors. Green light mixed with violet light also produces white or gray. Violet light is a mixture of red light and blue light.

Complementary Colors

A complementary color is the color a normal eye will see when closed or looking at a blank white sheet of paper after staring at a given radiant color. If a person stares at red they will see a greenish blue with the eyes closed. If they stare at orange they will see a deep blue. If they stare at yellow, they see a color between blue and violet. If they stare at greenish yellow, they will see a violet; and if at green, they will see magenta. If they reverse these colors and stare at greenish-blue, they will see red and so on.

Complementary Spectral Colors:

Red & Green
Orange & Blue
Yellow & Violet

The reason for this phenomenon seems to be that certain of the rods and cones in the retina, which are in tune with the color that is stared at, become fatigued and call up a sympathetic action of the nerves not acted upon. This sympathetic reaction will show up ten to sixty seconds depending upon the radiance and the person.

There are many mixtures of light that look white or gray. Some of them, like those reflected from a gray surface bathed in sunlight, include all the colors of the spectrum. There are others that include only two colors. Two colors which produce white or gray when light of these colors is mixed are called complementary colors. Such colors set each other off and serve especially well for purposes of contrast.

Pigments & Colored Light

Mixing light of different colors is not the same as mixing paints. For example, every artist knows that a mixture of blue and yellow paints makes green. Paints, dyes, and other coloring materials are able to take away certain wavelengths from the white light that falls on them, leaving only some of the wavelengths to be reflected. This taking up of certain colors is called absorption.

If you mix the proper amounts of paints of all possible colors, you get black paint. Each kind of coloring matter in the mixture absorbs its own set of wavelengths and nothing is left to be reflected. Anything that reflects very little light of any kind looks black and anything that reflects a mixture of many different wavelengths looks white. Black is not a color, but the absence of color, or the absence of reflected light.

Pigment soaks up certain color waves and reflects the rest of them. When you see a red building, or a red cloth, the pigment in the paint absorbs all the colors except red. Thus red is reflected to your eyes. A paint pigment is named for the color that it does not absorb. Plants look green because the material in them takes up almost every other color, and only the green is reflected and reaches your eyes.

The flakes of coloring matter in white paint may not be white at all. Under a microscope, these flakes may look as clear and colorless as glass, but because they reflect daylight so well, the paint looks white. Snow, which consists of colorless crystals of ice looks white for the same reason.

In blending pigment color, the subtractive process applies. When a painter mixes two pigment colors together, he is subtracting colors. The pigment in each color is like a filter that removes some colors from white light. In paints, inks and dyes, the primary colors are magenta, yellow and cyan. They are called primary because every other color can be produced by mixing them together in various portions or by adding white, gray or black to them.

In blending colored light, you add colors, the additive process. When a blue spotlight and a yellow spotlight shine on the same white surface, this kind of mixture is called additive, because it is made by adding one kind of light to another. Additive primaries are said to be red, green and blue. One color wheel uses orange, green and blue. This is based on mixing actual light rays, adding colors together. As white is the effect produced by all colors of light shining together, there will be a space of white at the center where the colors blend.

Color filters transmit light, but strain out certain colors and let others pass through. Most filters are made of glass or plastics, and these work by taking up part of the light passing through them. Traffic lights are a practical example. Most of the things we see around us are opaque and do not allow light to pass through at all. All the light that falls on them is either absorbed or reflected. If the object absorbs some colors and reflects others, then it looks colored. Its color is the color of the light it reflects, as the color of a filter is the color of the light it transmits.

THE IMPORTANCE OF MIND IN COLOR THERAPY

The sense of seeing is most important of the senses, though we see nothing really.

We see all of life in pictures. We know more of life through pictures than any other thing.

All our thoughts form mental pictures. Words form mental pictures and once the picture is formed, the judgment can be made.

You have never seen an object in the world. You have only seen a reproduction in your mind. Neither you nor anyone else knows how anything looks in the world, they have never seen it. All you have seen is electro-chemical interchange reproductions in your mind.

The only seeing is spiritually and it isn't done with the eyes.

Even medicine is coming to recognize the mental and emotional aspects of illnesses and is attempting to treat them as well as the physical. Color influences all of them, physical, emotional, mental and spiritual and can thus be used to affect the complete harmony which means perfect health.

Color is a force that can be used to produce definite effects even though the force is so gentle we cannot feel it. It can change the vibratory rate of different parts of the body. To understand this it is necessary to know that the physical body has an etheric counterpart or etheric body. This permeates the entire body and extends a little beyond it, being the matrix upon which the cells of the physical body are fitted. This etheric body has an aura which can be seen by some sensitives and it has shape, density, and texture which varies with the individual. It has its own rates of vibration and these are affected by color treatments.

That the finer vibrations in nature are of value in attacking disease has been realized by the homeopaths who work with minute doses. The mind of the patient is somewhat relieved as soon as he knows someone is going to help him. His emotional tension relaxes to an extent and nature has a better chance to put its forces to work and recuperate him.

Any interference in the harmony of the body, whether it is a lesion or an infection, sets forces of nature into action. All manifestation is produced by the Universal Mind, including the individual mind. The more the individual mind can be brought into harmony with the Universal Mind, the more quickly the healing can take place. No emotion or feeling which causes depression, fear, envy, worry, hatred, malice, anger can be permitted if health is desired for they are all destructive forces which break down the body. Until some control is obtained over the mind, progress towards health will be slow. It is worthwhile building up a good character if only from the selfish standpoint of health.

The plasticity of the mind is a factor that is of extreme utility in the process of regaining lost health, and we can whittle away at all these weaknesses, obtaining control over them little by little. Every time we entertain a mental concept we strengthen it and the repetition of a constructive thought will crowd out destructive or negative ones.

Fear is one of the first energies to be banished if we would be impregnable to the assaults of disease. Doubt is another. Cultivation of the imagination is the next step, picturing in the mind's eye the result desired. In health, the incessant movement of atoms is rhythmic, harmonious; in ill health it is discordant and inharmonious. Vibrations can be altered in character by thought or the power of mind. Mind is more highly organized than ordinary matter and matter is subservient to it, just as the muscular system is subservient to the will.

The final factor in color healing is the will. There must be the determination to throw off the yoke of disease, backing up the imagination and the throwing off of doubts and fear. At some fixed hour, preferably in the morning first thing, sit in a comfortable position in a chair and quiet the mind as much as possible. Then make a definite statement that you are the master of your body and disease and suffering cannot approach you. Visualize perfect health in every part, at your command. Continual repetition of this will in time bring conviction and the desired condition of health. And yet the realm of color cannot be conquered by intellect alone; it must also be grasped through feeling. One more aid, which can be used in conjunction with color healing, is charging the subconscious mind upon going to sleep at night, with the idea of health. Words are used to clothe thought.

Every variation of light and sound possesses its individual frequencies of radiation. They are a form of characterized energy, as is everything else in the universe. If one creates a known light frequency, the corresponding shade of light will appear. Similarly, each positive thought will possess its own definite energy formation.

Sound frequencies travel at a much lower velocity than that of light, taking five seconds to travel a mile through air. The frequency increases from the lowest pitch to the highest. Within the range of normal hearing each minute variation of the frequency has a different characterization. If the frequencies are sped up beyond the capacity of human ears to hear, there is still sound, which some animals can perceive. Continue to speed up the frequency and it will eventually be registered as a light experience, commencing with the infrared, and as the ultraviolet and beyond. It is remarkable that our organs of sense are geared to receive these high rates of energy vibration as human experiences. Continue the speeding up of the frequencies very much higher and they begin to enter into the range of thought, which again is recordable by the consciousness. So, just as every variation of sound and every refraction of light have its definite form, every thought has its set form capable of being recorded.

If thoughts were intangible, possessing no ordered form, they could not be filed away in the memory and revived when needed. The brain cannot record nothingness. Thought must be tangible. The number of recorded thoughts within the memory is incalculable. It is said that no thought is ever lost and that under hypnosis, the mind can be induced to bring forth memories of the past that could not have been consciously aroused.

It is logical that when a patient's mind is strongly obsessed with the incidents of disharmony it may be incapable of directly accepting a remedial influence. With the existence of a close condition of attunement between the healer and the patient, the healing directive is passed to the patient's bodily intelligence. There are much finer energies in the sunlight than those the ordinary eye can perceive as the blue and violet colors, and also finer energies in the forces of man, whose penetrating power as possessed by some persons, has brought marvelous help to many. For some persons are endowed with a magnetic healing touch. This differs from spiritual healing.

METHODS OF TREATMENT

Color Therapy with Glass

We have seen that the whole range of forces from the warmest to the most electrical, is to be found in the solar spectrum, and these forces are signified by the color. How shall we collect and store up these penetrating color forces fresh from the great fountain? Light is a substance as well as a motion and the color rays that constitute light are substances with chemical and therapeutic potencies. These rays may be strained off most conveniently by colored panes of glass that transmit certain rays that are required, and absorb the others.

For color therapy, several sheets of colored glass are required. Red, dark blue, yellow, orange, violet and green are the most useful. The sheets should be about ten by twelve inches. If there are definite symptoms a single sheet of one color may suffice. The glass may be placed in a picture frame of the right size, or the glass cut to the size of a frame. Or the glass may simply be hung up by means of a string in the window where the sun comes in.

Sitting in the light for twenty minutes to an hour constitutes a sunbath. Sunbaths are advocated at all periods of the year whenever it is possible to take one. If towards noon or the summer months, the head can be protected by a wet bandage or hat and little blue glass can be used over the heart. When a color is used, it is a color bath. If red glass, the head must be protected from the sun during hot weather.

Outdoor treatments, where the sun comes through the required color of glass, are recommended. Large panes of glass are best for this and these can be supported on a stand about four feet from the ground, arranged so that the patient can lie under it comfortably. Following the idea for the ancients with their solaria on the roofs of their houses, a solarium can also be built on the roof or in the attic for colored glass to be arranged overhead, so that it will be exposed to the sun all day. Children may be sent to play in the solarium to gain power, purity of blood and activity of the skin.

The healing powers of the colors in glass are somewhat different from their appearance to the eye as can be perceived when tested by a prism. Red for instance is the hottest visible color but red glass does not transmit as much heat as orange or even yellow glass. The power to transmit color must therefore be considered, not the visual effect.

Different kinds of glass transmit different powers of color. The blue glass transmits not only blue, but other colors in the spectrum, both hot and cold, visible and invisible. The yellow ray is absent and much of the green. Orange and red are partially transmitted. The infrared rays pass through blue. For calming and cooling the brain, nerves and inflammatory actions blue is unexcelled. Blue light is certain death to bacteria. But it should not be used in any disease where there are symptoms of expended vitality or exhaustion. To determine if a glass is the mazarine blue, hold a lighted match or lamp just back of it and it will have a violet tint; if it remains blue the same as before, it is not mazarine but a cooled grade of blue. Blue glass in the sun becomes heated by the warm rays it absorbs, but the rays which it transmits are cooling.

Many other combinations both in glass and solutions are possible. Heat is transmitted by red glass, but the orange glass admitting a small amount of electric rays seems to produce even more heat. Red glass should be used where there is a general lack of virility, a want of tone, with anemia, or cold melancholia. The warm colors such a red, orange and yellow are suited to the lower part of the body. If it is necessary to use them on the upper portion, they should not rest over the heart for too long at a time. Red is not to be used where there is an excited condition of an organ or the mind.

Light Source Lamps

A full spectrum lamp is a good alternative to the sunlight for use indoors and during cloudy weather. Mount the color lamp two to six feet from the area to be irradiated, or hang it on the wall directly above and midway of the bed if the lamp is so designed. From this angle it can be trained easily in all directions and is out of the way.

A deep therapy lamp produces radiant light and heat. Its action upon the general metabolism of the body is as follows: first, the oxygen-carrying function of the blood is increased by a greater percentage of hemoglobin on account of the direct action of the irradiation of the light rays. There is a stimulation of the lymphatic system and increased elimination of waste products by the sudoriferous glands and other excretory organs of the body. The treatment replicates sunlight as closely as possible. We have a solar spectrum and its 7 octaves of color; we have ultraviolet and infrared rays.

Light treatment is indicated for use in acute as well as chronic diseases. It first raises the temperature by the absorption of the infrared rays into the blood stream and then reduces the temperature through its action upon the oxidation and excretory processes of the body, eliminating the toxins and stimulating the metabolic functions.

Charging Water

In addition to sunbathing under colored glass, it is very beneficial to use water that has been exposed to the color rays. Such water can be taken either internally or used for washing or bathing. To prepare this water take clear glass bottles free from any tint. Fill the bottles with water and place them on the windowsill behind the sheets of colored glass; smaller strips of glass can be used. Instead of using the color glass, the bottles may be of glass in the desired colors. Only vibrant transparent colors may be used, nothing cloudy, milky or dull.

To charge water, place bottles of different colors filled with pure water in the sun for at least one hour. Several hours will charge it more strongly than one hour. In cold weather remember not to let it freeze and break the bottles. The blue, being an antiseptic principle, prevents the water from becoming putrid, however long it may stand, but the red and yellow had best be changed every two or three weeks at least in cold weather, and every three or four days in warm weather. The violet water remains pure a long time.

Filtered water is more apt to generate bacteria than unfiltered, but it may be used in the bottles if not allowed to stand more than three days. The same applies to boiled water. Ordinary water treated with color will keep a couple of weeks in a temperature of sixty degrees. But as a couple of hours of strong sunlight is sufficient to impregnate the water there is no need to keep it beyond a few days.

If a large bottle, or a number of bottles can be light exposed, a bath in this water will be found very effectual where tone is lacking. If there is not enough water for the bath, a sponge-down in the radiated water will be helpful. Clothing exposed to these colored rays has a therapeutic effect according to the color employed. The beneficial results of a sunbath will be enhanced by wearing light and airy clothes. When practicable, the naked skin should receive the rays.

Charging Other Substances

Food or medicines are capable of transmitting the potency of the rays if exposed a short time to them. No taste of the color is perceptible, except to sensitives and this is a pleasant way of absorbing the radiation. The color forces can be conveyed most readily to water as the most neutral and best balanced substance in nature and the most convenient for use. Sugar of milk, or the smaller grade of homeopathic pellets of sugar, are another choice. Sugar of milk, which is best for charging without becoming lumpy, should be coarse and granulated.

To charge sugar pellets, sugar of milk, etc., spread the material out thin in a small vial of the desired color. These constitute medicines and should be kept in vials of the same color, or if these are not conveniently found, in cloth or paper of the same color, and should be kept in the sun as much as possible. Solarized materials are most active when taken directly from the sun but will retain the same kind of power for some time.

To get absolutely pure violet or any violet-charged substance, it will be necessary to expose the substance to the violet rays as separated by a prism in a camera obscura. Blue bottles or lenses would almost equal violet for soothing nerves, and surpass it for cooling the blood. The doses for these solar medicines can be taken in the form of color-charged water, two to four swallows, or about three tablespoons at a time, or two teaspoons for little children.

A family that is constipated may amberize their bread a few minutes by placing it in the sun under amber glass and thus find relief. Or a person who has irritation of the stomach and bowels may place their food in the sun under blue glass. Wine becomes more or less amberized, and thus animating in its nature, by being put into yellow bottles as is so commonly done.

Substances charged by the full white light receives a vitalizing force. Some delicate people cannot drink ordinary cold water, but if such water could stand in the sun awhile, it is probable that almost anyone however feeble could drink it. Abundant exposure to the sun will give a great increase in magnetic power.

Gases, such as the atmosphere, may also be color charged and the lungs can be reached. The air in a red bottle will become rubified by moments in the sun, and if inhaled as soon as the cork drawn, will prove animating to the bronchi and lungs. In a blue bottle, it will be healing and soothing to irritated or hemorrhage conditions of the lungs or phthisis.

The power of these sun-charged substances has been tested hundreds of times and in many cases they have proved marvelously effective when all drugs and other remedies have failed. They are especially gentle, safe, far-reaching and enduring in their effect.

TREATMENT WITH COLOR

Basic Effects of Colors

Red, yellow and orange tire us and irritate us sooner than the other colors. They are heat producing and exciting. A quiet, relaxed person will be excited and irritated by bright improperly handled colors. These colors also make a room seem smaller. They are animating, stimulating and warming.

Blue, green and violet are cool and soothing. A nervous, quick moving person is calmed by blues, greens and violets. These make a room seem larger. People underestimate the temperature of a blue room and overestimate that of a red room. They overestimate the passage of time under the influence of red and underestimate it under the influence of blue.

Green walls make meat look redder than ever. Yellow walls make meat have a gray after-image, robbing it of the natural redness. Muscle reactions are faster under red light and slower under green light. Darker colored objects are perceived to be heavier than light colored objects. Blue is more visible at night and red is more visible during the daytime.

Sunlight and Medications

In healing by color, the subtlest and finest vibrations in nature are used instead of the coarse irritating vibrations of drugs and chemicals. The reason drugs work is because of the free electrons which they give off. The rest of the compound is useless to the system and must be eliminated. In the process of ridding the body of this unwanted matter, damage is done to the system that also has to be corrected. Therefore, the drug used for the cure just traded one problem for another.

When a drug is taken into the body it is carried by the blood stream to that organ or part of the body in accordance with its particular make-up. The drugged part or organ struggles to expel the drug and is thus stimulated or slowed down so that the normal rate of vibration can be restored. In many cases, however, the disturbed rate of psychic vibration is aggravated, hence the effect of the drug is uncertain and often leaves the patient in a worse condition. The homeopath only uses a small dosage that has been attenuated to perhaps one part in a million, so there is not much residue. Should the physician consider drugs necessary, the color healing will not interfere with their use, though it is preferable that herbal decoctions be used. But practice and experience show that the rays of the sun carry all the elements needed to re-establish and maintain the health of the body.

Sunlight carries the energy that establishes normal vibrations and it will restore abnormal vibrations back to normal when properly employed. The radiations of sunlight are absorbed by the nervous system and distributed by it and the blood stream to various parts of the body. When the body is in a normal condition it can filter from the white light of the sun whatever color vibration it may need. The Sun's rays are so powerful that they will cauterize a vein or an artery and almost instantaneously stop the bleeding. No after dressing is needed except in the case of cancer. As the Sun's rays are not poisonous there are no bad after affects as with the use of drugs. There are no preparations necessary but the operator can cauterize as deeply as may be needed with no scarring left after the healing is completed. Augustus Barnes removed cancers in their earlier stages, tumors, moles and birthmarks no matter what the size or color. He used the lens and the simple rays of the Sun without any bleeding or a permanent scar.

When a body is in a morbid state, it is much more easily restored to normal by having specific parts of the sunlight applied by means of color filters or screens. This is the science of color therapy that applies specific colors to change morbid vibrations into normal healthy vibrations.

General Recommendations

Color is the most attenuated form of energy that can be kept in an individual state that will do the work that needs to be done and leave no residue, as it is all free energy. There is no residue to contaminate the body, and it is the residue that keeps the body from being healthy. Colors are harmless and normalizing in their effect on the body. However, if the process of loosening and eliminating of toxins and congestions from the body occurs too rapidly, one might feel upset. Do not stop treatment unless the condition becomes unbearable. If the treatment causes extreme pain or dizziness that does not go away soon, then use turquoise for temporary relief.

The colors must be irradiated on the bare skin in a dark room. The room should be comfortably warm during the treatment. The treatment may be taken with the head to the North and the feet to the South and it is best to be in a reclining position. Complete relaxation is important and it is desirable to remain so for a short time after the treatment period. During treatment, avoid those things that cause toxic effects, such as meat, coffee, tobacco and alcoholic beverages. They slow down the natural processes of the body to build new and healthy tissues and cells and retard the natural processes of the eliminative organs to remove mucous poisons and waste from the body, thus interfering with nature's efforts to heal. All forms of refined and devitalized foods should also be eliminated as they are dead and therefore cannot build live and healthy tissues. Drink plenty of water and fruit juices as they flush out the body and dissolve waste. It is especially helpful to drink one half lemon in a glass of lukewarm water. For sweetening use honey, or the type of molasses that does not contain sulfur dioxide. Pure maple syrup may be used instead of molasses with good results as it down not have the laxative effect of molasses.

Any color treatment should be accompanied by attention to diet, sleep, bathing, breathing, exercise and general hygiene. Generally wait two hours after eating a meal before taking a treatment. It is permissible to use color directly after a full meal if there is indigestion, gas or other distress. Yellow is indicated in this event.

Emergency treatment may be taken at any time of day or night as long as it necessary to obtain the desired results. For best results, wait at least two hours between treatments. Ordinarily do not take these treatments during the sunrise or sunset period. Also do not take them during an eclipse of the Sun or Moon.

The specific parts of the body to which color treatment is applied are the head, forehead, and nape of the neck, the whole spine, the solar plexus at the end of the breastbone and the corresponding region of the spine, the chest, the lumbar region above the loins and the abdomen. The nerve centers, particularly the spine and solar plexus, are the most important points for treatment. If there is a local ailment the treatment can be applied to that, but the general strengthening of the entire system is necessary as well. When there are local ailments such as facial neuralgia, nasal catarrh, eye trouble, rheumatism in the joints, or constipation, color treatment may be given directly to these parts.

A general treatment should also be given to tone up the whole body at the same time because if any part of the body has congested or deficient disorders, the rest of the body is affected. We must always consider the overall picture when correcting any disorder. It should be seen that the bowels move freely and the blood should be vitalized, which can be accomplished by using violet over the liver, stomach and lungs, along with outdoor sunlight, pure air and simple nourishing food. The healing powers of light and color are so gentle, so penetrating, so enduring and often potent when coarser methods are ineffective. The action of color treatment is so gentle as at times to be almost imperceptible, taking sometimes two, six, twelve or twenty-four hours.

Two Methods of Diagnosis

There are two methods of diagnosis, seeing the cause and detecting the symptoms. The first method is possible for those who have developed color awareness or clairvoyant vision. The second is mainly physical.

Beyond the physical body is the spiritual body, and some have claimed as many as seven subtle bodies each of which radiates waves of color. The clairvoyant observes these colors and from them can discern the area the deficiency is located, thus showing the cause of the illness. At first it will be difficult to distinguish between the color of rest and the color of activity. The latter has a vital sparkling appearance, the rest color has a smoothly flowing serene quality. More about the colors of the body will be discussed in the chapter on visualization.

The physical method of diagnosis is obtained by observing the patient's manner of movement and general appearance. If he is lacking in red, for instance, he would seem lazy, anemic, sluggish, lacking in appetite and constipated. If lacking in blue, he would be hot-headed, active and inclined to feverishness. In this broad diagnosis there are but two colors to be considered, the two opposites, the heating red and the cooling blue-violet. Green is the middle or balancing point. Four physical things about a person help to show what color is lacking: the color of the eyeballs, nails, urine and bowels. The color of all four should be taken into consideration as one alone may be deceptive. The eyes may appear red and yet the system as a whole may need more red.

In treating an individual, it is first necessary to determine his type. If excitable, nervous, or passionate in nature, the soothing colors blue, violet or green are to be used. If the lymphatic bilious temperament, the individual requires red, orange and yellow. The color which the individual lacks is the one which should be applied.

Breathing

Next in importance, attention should be paid to breathing. Pure blood is necessary for the body to be healthy. Without fresh air and plenty of it, it is impossible to make this fluid pure. Fresh air must not only be breathed for a few hours every day, but it must be admitted into the house, the bedroom, the office and wherever suited. If one is forced to be in a stuffy room, shorter breaths should be taken so as to take as little of it as possible into the lungs before getting into the fresh air. Though it may not be advisable in cold weather to admit fresh air during daytime due to chill or draft, the bedroom should always be ventilated to some extent while one sleeps.

There is an art of breathing. First, breathe always through the nose. Second, put the shoulders back, close the lips and commence to inhale slowly, at the rate of about eight inhalations a minute. Do this about twenty times a day at first, then try to do it habitually unless exercising takes care of this. As correct breathing is an important part of health, the patient should be given instructions regarding it while under treatment. The normal person takes more time to exhale than inhale, that is, there is a slight lull after exhalation.

During treatment breathe by diaphragm only. In this manner the chest being elevated has to be filled before the air can push the diaphragm downwards. As it is pushed down, elevate the abdomen. This is true diaphragm breathing and the only way anyone should breathe. The rhythm in breathing sets the pace of the heart and all the capillary movements of the entire body, including the interchange of body fluids and internal secretions.

Length of Exposure

Experience and judgment are needed in determining the length of exposure in every case. Overexposure, however, is rarely a serious matter except in those few instances that have been noted. An overdose of color is not like an overdose of a drug that may be a poison. Should it be felt that an overdose of color has been given, it can be remedied by using the complementary color to the one previously used. An overdose of yellow, for instance, can be corrected by a short exposure to violet or blue. However, an exposure to the wrong color is not always so easily rectified, for if yellow were mistakenly applied in the case of heat and inflammation, a subsequent exposure to blue might not put it entirely right.

In judging the right length of exposure for any color, a number of factors have to be taken into consideration – the climactic and weather conditions, the time of year, the hour of the day, the color and the density of the color filter, the nature and extent of disease, and finally the sensitiveness and response of the individual.

Exposure to the bright sun of May, June and July, for instance, would be doubled or tripled if the day were cloudy. Do not bathe during the hot noonday sun in midsummer. In March, April, August or September when the sun's rays are slanted lower, the length of exposure would be increased. Use common sense on such matters.

Some colors require a longer exposure than others. Red and yellow have a quicker visible effect on the skin than blue or violet, but they require a longer exposure than blue or violet. Blue and violet are powerful in their chemical, electric and psychic effects. It is to be remembered that red draws the arterial blood to the surface and consequently reddens the skin, whereas blue sends the blood inwards. Blue on an inflamed surface will blanch it, reducing the heat and easing the pain, and this usually takes place more quickly than the heating or stimulating of yellow.

A few typical exposure times are listed here as a general guide, as the length of the exposure varies according to the illness and the response of the patient. For ordinary purposes, irradiations should last from five minutes to one hour. More than one hour at a time can cause no harm, but usually one hour is sufficient.

Abdomen: 10-60 minutes
Chest: 10-30 minutes
Constipation (yellow): 10-30 minutes
Diarrhea (blue): 15-60 minutes
Nasal catarrh (blue): 5-15 minutes
Neuralgia (blue): 10-30 minutes
Rheumatism in joints (blue): 10-30 minutes
Sciatica: 30 minutes to 2 hours
Solar plexus: 5-20 minutes
Stomach: 5-20 minutes

These are diffused sunlight exposures given near a window. Exposure in bright direct sunlight would cut these times by one half or a third. If a long exposure is required the glass can be placed in a frame on a stand. But frequent short exposures are generally more effective than a continuous long one which is apt to be tiring and therefore less effective. In giving the treatment, the glass is not to touch the body.

Rhythmic Interrupted Radiant Light Method

Every disease causes the body to give off energy. The energies differ as the diseases differ. All of these energies have color. The diseased condition in the body can therefore be identified by the color it gives off. It is necessary to know the colors that are complementary to each other in healing work as opposites have a more powerful effect when used alternately, greatly increasing the metabolism. This works on the same principle as hydropathic use of hot and cold water alternately. When a complementary color is applied, it interferes with the disease radiations and tends to cause a permanent rest of the disease.

Some therapists very much favor connecting an interrupting device to the deep therapy lamp so that the light is interrupted on and off with a rhythmical frequency. This interrupting device increases the therapeutic value of the light fifty percent, because with the interruption of the current a magnetic field is created about the patient as the light goes off.

With the interrupted light there is an expansion and contraction of the capillaries and a massage action of the tissues. The interruption should be done in accord with the rhythm of the patient's pulse or breathing, and also in accord with the type of the individual. The patient with low blood pressure is weak and anemic and gets along better with a rapid rhythmic interruption. Slow interruption is better for those with high blood pressure, and also for sedation.

A further increase in the effectiveness of the color treatment is gained by using the indicated color while the patient is inhaling, and the complementary color while exhaling.

The effect of red, for instance, is greatly increased by the use of its complementary color green; of yellow by the alternate use of its complementary color violet, and so on. If red be the indicated color, the red is tuned to the patient's natural rhythm and she inhales while the red radiates on her bared chest or body. Then the green is tuned to her rhythm and radiates on her while she exhales.

Each individual has a normal rhythm, but it is changed when there is some unrest of tissue in the body. The rhythm may be too rapid or it may be too slow, or it may be out of correct periodicity. The average ration of inhaling to exhaling is between forty to sixty and forty-four to fifty-six. The cycle of respiration averages from seven to twelve, when the patient is lying on the table or couch.

At the beginning of the treatment the patient's rhythm is recorded on the card and the first one or two treatments or sometimes more. As the patient's condition becomes more normal, the rhythm will be found to change and the timing of the alternating color radiations will also have to be changed. The beginning of one treatment, however, will be timed the same as the ending of the previous treatment.

When the first color has been given for twenty-five minutes on the front of the body, the complementary color is given for about fifteen minutes. The patient lies on the table face up and inhales while the indicated color is radiated on the epigastric regions and chest, then exhales while the complementary color is radiated on the body.

TREATMENT VISUALIZATIONS

Visualization of the Healer

A darkened room is used with the patient seated in a comfortable chair or relaxed on a couch with the lamp placed behind or to the side so that the rays do not shine directly into his eyes. He should be bared to the waist (or chest draped for women) if convenient. The healer sits beside the patient and gets him to relax and let his mind dwell on the color being used, then closes his eyes. He may be able to see a color in front of his closed lids, which may at first be the color complementary to the one being used, but the latter will soon appear.

He must remain relaxed and not use his will but rather his imagination. The healer places his right hand on the patient, either on the head, wrist or the affected part in order to become in rapport with him. He now uses his will to send the color into the patient. When used in this way the color acts upon the etheric body. If the healer has clairvoyance, he will see the color entering the patient and changing the color in the etheric body; or he may be able to sense it or make a mental picture of the color as clear and sparkling, recharging the cells from the head downward.

If the condition is functional or nervous, recharging alone will fill the exhausted nerve cells. If there is disease with loss of tissue, the etheric body has been damaged and must be restored so the physical cells can build into the pattern. The healer must visualize the color filling the damaged part and restoring it. This must be done on all planes, visualizing the mental building the etheric, and the etheric, the gross physical. The powers of creative imagination must be used both by the healer and the patient. This calls up the healing force within the individual and the healer's creative force is added to it. The healer thus tunes himself to color and this mode of motion is the keynote that accomplishes the healing.

In most cases three colors are used, green, blue and orange, according to the healing required. They may be employed at one sitting or at different ones. The green is used if calming is the objective, then may be followed by the others, the green and blue about ten minutes each and the orange not more than five minutes. The total time of a treatment can be a half hour or more according to the colors used.

Color Breathing

Permanent results in healing can only be obtained if the patient is able to cooperate. There are ways in which he can be helped to do this. One is through instruction in color breathing.

To practice color breathing the patient visualizes the color pouring upon him while under the treatment lamp and for a few moments beforehand. He should also do this upon arising in the morning and on retiring at night and be as open during the day as possible. As he inhales he visualizes the color entering the body and mind as eagerly as a breath of fresh air is drawn in after being in a closed room. A simple mantra spoken or thought at the same time adds to the definiteness of the results; the affirmation should be tuned in to the color vibration.

The ordinary breath draws from the surrounding atmosphere those things the body needs to continue living; and it expels into the atmosphere those things the body no longer needs. When this is done consciously and linked up with the larger cosmic atmosphere the finer forces can be drawn in and will supply whatever we want on all planes. We should therefore make the conscious effort to expel with the breath the dead and useless things from our bodies gathered through wrong living, thinking and feeling.

If red, orange or yellow is being used in the color treatment, they should be visualized as being drawn up from the earth through the soles of the feet. When blue, indigo or violet is the treatment color, visualize the color coming in horizontally as from the green countryside.

Colors of the Body

When there is illness in the body tissues, from errors that have come on gradually in eating or living habits, the subconscious mind does not report it to the conscious mind until there is a condition that alarms all the metabolic processes. The individual then knows something is wrong but not where the trouble is. If a sudden accelerated flow of blood were established through the diseased part, as though a fog had been blown away, the location of the affected tissue would stand out. In this way, rhythmic color treatment enables the patient to tell what she feels and the seat of the trouble is verified. The same rhythm that locates the trouble will rectify the abnormal condition and establish ease in place of disease.

Often the color that causes a strange feeling to subside quickly tells what the disease is. For example, ruby indicates tuberculosis and cancer. Many thousands of cases have been tested with the ruby light, with no disease found except tuberculosis and cancer that would respond to that color. Tuberculosis could be diagnosed by this method at the very inception of the disease, and before a diagnosis could be made by any other known method. Blue indicates syphilis or autointoxication; violet, gonorrheal conditions; orange, cancerous; green, hepatic intoxication. But even if no name is known to give the distressed condition, the treatment will be the same. Remember that not forty percent of regular diagnoses given by the average doctor are correct; the name of the disorder means little as it is not the name that is being treated, but the disorder.

Colors also produce a far-reaching effect upon the development of all forms of life. Bacilli when exposed to ultraviolet rays are changed into a different species. Every unit of matter throughout the universe, whether it is a unit of mercury or a unit of gold, silver, copper, tin, iron, or salt has its distinctive color. It is true that all of the mineral elements give off various colors, which constitute their individual spectrums; nevertheless, there is one part of the spectrum of color which is most definite for each element and this is known as the distinct color of that piece of matter.

People with spiritual sight have noted that the various organs and parts of the body have their specific color vibrations. In the lungs, orange and red are well developed and to some extent the yellow. In the stomach, the ruling color is yellow, with a sufficient amount of blue to give it a yellow green cast. The sexual organs are surrounded by a reddish brown, being a darker cast than the region of amativeness in the head. The heart has been seen as a deep red. The bowels are yellow, with the lower part greenish mixed with some red. The lower back brain is a dark red, which merges gradually into bluish white as we move down the spine.

The spine is bluish white as the ruling color, with also a reddish-brown cast at the lower part. The whole nervous system shows streams of bluish white light coursing all through its channels. The arteries exhibit currents of red light and the veins a grade of color less luminous than the arteries. Around the solar plexus, all the colors radiate in a brilliant rainbow style. A magnetic hand placed at that spot would have a healing effect on all below it but not so much above. A considerable variety of color is seen in the region of the hypogastric plexus. The feet send out quite a variety of colors, the warm colors predominant.

The head being the opposite pole of the body sends out a variety of colors with blue predominating, especially at the back and front upper portions. The psychic colors of the brain as seen by a developed sensitive are as follows: At the base of the brain in back, the animal lobes, the colors are a dark red, and in persons of a very low nature almost black. In the upper brain the colors assume a yellowish tint and are far more brilliant. In a high nature, the colors of the moral and spiritual powers are almost dazzling, with the yellow tint nearly merged into white, and far more exquisite than sunlight. In the higher front brain, the region of the reasoning intellect, blue is the predominant color, and is lighter as it approaches the top brain, darker as it comes down to the perceptive powers, over the brow, with a little touch of violet in its outer edges.

Benevolence emits a soft green light of indescribable beauty. Over-firmness, the color is scarlet and over self-esteem. Moving down the sides of the head from the moral powers at the top towards the lower lobes, the colors become orange, then red, then dark at the bottom. Very low natures sometimes emit such a dark cloud from the base of the brain that they can scarcely be seen by the psychic. When a person laughs or sends forth happy thoughts it causes a dancing play of bright colors; but when in violent passion, a snapping and sparkling red is emitted.

Firmness is seen by some as blue rather than scarlet. Firmness seems to form the upper end of a mass of polarized lines of force which run down through the whole spine and thus, when active, causes the whole being to become braced up into a rigid and powerful condition, hence the effect which we call firmness. These firm conditions or polarizations come from energies that have the blue principle.

The eyes, perceptive and reasoning powers radiate blue emanations; animal energies including amativeness or sexual love are red. Religion is yellow. The blue of the reasoning powers is a grade higher than the blue of firmness, the red of the front lower face is finer and more brilliant than that of the back hand, and the red of the more celestial grade of love is higher than the psychic, as is the yellow of religion or veneration. The nose has a green emanation, the lips yellow, below the lips orange, the chin scarlet, the temporal region violet, merging into the finer red above and the coarser red below. Violet in this section includes idealism and sublimity.

All the colors appear more pure and brilliant as they approach the upper brain, and are far more magnificent in a high and noble nature than in a low and selfish one. The region of religious aspiration is the most luminous of all and in a person of noble and spiritual nature, an exquisite golden yellow approaches a pure and dazzling white.

The perception of these finer ethers can be developed by many people with a little practice. Get in touch with the patient's vibrations. If the body is suffering in any way, the vibrations of the life energy in the blood and nerves will be inharmonious and the patient will be out of tune.

Hands on Practice

Have the patient sit in a chair. Clasp the patient's right hand with your palm in contact with his. Then close your eyes very tightly to keep light out of your eyes, and concentrate your mind on them. Wait patiently until you see some faint lights in your eyes. The lights will appear hazy and dull or very soft – and will seem to be all over the inside of your eyelids. Sometimes it will seem as though you were looking into a large mirror that slowly passes into a faint glow or hazy tint. It will take two or three minutes at first for you to see even the lightest tint. It may take several days practice before you can see these lights; some will be able to see these lights the moment they touch a person's hand, even with the eyes only partly closed.

The lights that appear are the colors of the spectrum, caused by the vibrations from the person's hand entering your hand and passing up the radial nerve of the arm to the sympathetic nervous system. The colors you will see are: blue, green, yellow, orange, red, and violet. They may appear one at a time in both eyes, or one color in one eye with another color in the other eye, or two colors at a time, or sometimes three. But seldom is more than one color seen and sometimes a great white light is seen.

When any color is seen, it indicates that the patient needs the complementary color. If a white light appears, the person may need both complementary colors. Give the positive (red, orange and yellow) treatment last, allowing a ten-minute interval after the negative one (green, blue, violet). Practice on anyone, because only about one person in a hundred is perfectly toned. Of course, you must not practice on a stranger, but someone in your own group who fully understands what you are doing, and will not take it personally.

The strength of the colors shows how lacking in vibrations the patient is. Five minutes of holding hands is the longest time usually necessary to see the lights. If no colors or white light appear you have not concentrated well. The same results could be had by placing the thumb and first finger of the right hand to the right of approximately the fourth cervical vertebra. This location is at the right side of the nape of the neck.

SPIRITUAL-PHYSICAL AFFIRMATIONS

Red

The universal breathing affirmation, which is to precede this, said by the patient as well as by the healer, can be accompanied by a visualization of the dawn or sunset on snowy mountain peaks as a warm or peachy pink spreading over the entire earth and all its inhabitants. The individual inhales the pink color and exhales the radiance and goodwill far over the horizon. Without goodwill the healing will not be permanent. The universal affirmation is:

> O Thou radiant spirit of divine love
> Enter my inner consciousness;
> O Thou spirit of divine love, dwell in my heart
> That love may make radiant
> Each thought, word, deed,
> Ever shining as my brother's beacon
> Radiating joy, peace, and power!

When the colored light treatment is given, the healer first of all surrounds the patient with the universal peachy tint. He asks the patient to cooperate by using the universal affirmation followed by the one for the red ray:

> O Ruby Rays, flow through me,
> Flow through me, and energize
> My bloodstream, my bloodstream.
>
> O Ruby Rays, stimulate activity, activity;
> And instill iron stamina, staunch stamina.
>
> O Ruby Rays, recharge my will
> With Thy goodwill,
> For health and joy

For me and all I will fulfill.

After the patient has cooperated in this way, he is placed on the couch under a sheet and the red light radiated upon the soles of his feet from a distance of about six inches. If the treatment is for anemia, a second color orange, is radiated upon the spleen area for thirty minutes.

On sunny days the noon sun power will be especially beneficial, focusing it on the soles of the feet through a red screen. At the same time the patient is to breathe in the ruby rays.

The treatment begins on the soles of the feet, then the lamp or the red screen is gradually moved to the ankles, the calves, the knees, the thighs and to the coccygeal center or chakra, remaining from five to ten minutes on each place. To end the treatment, green or blue is radiated on the patient for ten minutes so there may be no undesirable or irritating effects from the red.

The color treatment for paralysis is somewhat different from the above. Paralysis is usually due to shock or frustration of some kind wherein the patient is mentally or emotionally confused and, not knowing what step to take next, refuses to take any and the motor nerves cease to give orders. The patient needs some new and absorbing interest. Red gives an urge to action, strengthens willpower and courage. The adjustment of the mental attitude seems to take place more readily if the patient is unaware of its relation to the cure. Yellow is often helpful in treating the mentality in such a case. The patient is also given violet solarized water to drink between meals.

The violet is shone upon the patient lying face down on the couch, starting at the coccygeal chakra. After fifteen minutes on this spot the light is moved slowly up the spine to a position back of the solar plexus taking about five minutes to do it. Then the violet color is focused on the soles of the feet for fifteen minutes.

If the legs are paralyzed, focus the violet light on each sciatic nerve, playing it upon the back of the legs in an upward direction. Next change to the red light radiating it on the knees, shins, and feet for another ten minutes.

Indigo is to be used next, five minutes on the solar plexus then moved slowly to the throat center where it is held for five minutes and then changed to the blue light for ten minutes.

A complete cure will take three months or longer. The red rays can be discontinued in five to eight weeks, depending upon the severity of the case, as an overdose of the red, which stimulates adrenalin, would be harmful. In infantile paralysis the ruby shower should be employed by red light treatment.

Orange

In giving the orange color treatment the patient is asked to cooperate by visualizing the sun lighting and warming the earth and its children, at the same time breathing in its wisdom and light. The red part of the ray is sent to all parts of the physical body and the yellow to the mind. The red is giving strength and energy and the yellow makes the mind dynamic, alert and good-natured. Good nature toward all is essential in permanent health.

Accompanying this visualization the following affirmation is to be said:

> O freeing orange, O buoyant rays,
> Float in me, float in me,
> Salving, restoring conscious will,
> Conscious energy,
> Above all limits of bodily mind.
>
> O warming orange, dispel all chills
> And kindred ills; in me health thrills.

O lifting orange, transmuting rays,
Waken, unfold, my budding powers.
Bring me wisdom's bright new powers,
Bright new powers.

In practicing this affirmation, breathe from the pit of the stomach feeling as if the breath were coming from the feet. Breathe through the nostrils.

Yellow

The visualization before receiving the yellow light treatment consists in seeing golden currents of sun-radiant air flowing within the earth and enriching all the peoples of the world; see this golden light flowing into your body permeating every part of it. Do this first thing in the morning before an open window while taking about twenty deep breaths.

Following is the mantra to use with the yellow color breathing:

O yellow beams of gold, enrich my intelligence,
Strengthen thy sun-radiance, aged- wisdom
In youth unfold.

Empower my solar-plexus to digest, assimilate,
Inhaling golden atoms of joy,
All fear abates.

O saffron rays of wisdom prana
Flow in golden currency feeding cells
With cosmic manna throughout my entirety.

Yellow rays carry positive magnetic currents strengthening the nerves and awakening and vitalizing the mentality and reasoning faculties. They stimulate the third chakra at the solar plexus which controls the digestive processes. It has a cleansing and eliminative action on the liver, intestine and skin. Diseases which are benefitted by yellow color treatment include digestive and liver ailments, diabetes and skin diseases.

Green

The color breathing for green should be accompanied by the visualization of early morning light shimmering on dewy grass, the refreshing green of leaves after rain, the sun sparkling on shining trees at noon, green shadows at dusk dancing through the leaves, nature's prana.

Accompany this with the green ray affirmation:

> O Ray of emerald symphony, sustain, upbuild my wayward heart;
> Its strings attune in symphony, teach me to do my poiseful part.
>
> O chlorophyllic builder true, heart-force in fields and men renew.
> From thee the tempo true is bidden, O strengthen thou the beat, the rhythm.
>
> The pulse of brotherhood regain, bring forth the honey, harbored, hidden,
> In human hearts now freely given, sweet food in all, for all sustain.

Blue

In the color breathing for blue, visualize a cloudless bright blue sky of an early summer morning being breathed into the lungs and absorbed by every eager pore in the body. Think of yourself as sailing high above the earth and all the minute activities upon it, absorbed in the consciousness of blue. Then give the affirmation:

O tranquil ray of sapphire blue, calm thou my mind
In solace new, in solace new.
Quench thou all fevers in coolness new, refreshing dew.

Tone thou my speech, O ray of blue,
And make it true, and make it true.
Help me to learn, O ray of blue
To rest in you, to rest in you.
Help me to learn, O ray of blue,
To speak anew, to speak anew.
Help me to learn, O ray of blue,
To sing in you, to sing in you.

Indigo

Before giving the indigo ray affirmation in the color breathing, visualize the deep indigo of the desert midnight sky and drink deeply of it. Or imagine yourself in the deep indigo of a mountain lake, like an indigo trout inhabiting the lake, drinking deeply of the indigo waters which flow and ripple over your entire body and mind.

Then breathing rhythmically as you inhale and exhale the indigo use this affirmation:

O deep rays of indigo blue, bathe my eyes with tender hue.
Give me sight to see anew, give me light for seeing true.

O deep rays of indigo blue, bathe my ears with deeper hue
Tone my ears to hear anew, tune my mind to hearing true.

O deep rays of indigo blue, bring me in devotion's hours

The balm, the purity in mental showers release new
fragrance from brain flowers
Sweeping all brown leaves away.

Indigo is a great purifier of the blood stream and likewise
controls the psychic currents of the subtle bodies. It combines
the deep blue of devotion and clear thought with a faint trace of
stabilizing red. Great changes take place under its influence on
all levels of being. It is electric, cooling and astringent and can
induce local or total insensibility. But it enables the individual to
see and understand more deeply.

It governs the chakra in the center of the forehead called the
spiritual eye, controlling the pineal gland and vision, hearing
and smell on the physical and higher planes. Its complementary
color is yellow with which it has an affinity in regard to the mind.

Violet

For the color breathing of this hue, visualize the desert at sunset
being overspread with a mist of pure amethyst changing to deep
violet as dusk deepens. There is complete silence everywhere.
Breathe it in reverently feeling it penetrating every nerve fiber
and cell, nourishing and uplifting all spiritual life within.

Then use this affirmation while inhaling and exhaling deeply:

O zenith ray of violet power
Cleanse my dark blood with violet shower,
Soothe thou my nerves with passions lower,
Bring forth true inspiration's flower.

O amethyst ray of spirit's radiance,
Strike thou the chord of my soul's cadence
Bring forth the poetry, music fragrance
One art uniting – none in vagrancy.

O violet blaze in meditation's bower,
Flash me keen intuition's power,
Dull mental shades no more shall dower
Thy mystic petalled lotus flower.

The humble modest violet slight
Shows arrogance, power in simple might,
Guides egos from dark paths of night
In service selfless endless light.

THE COLOR RED

Red is the fundamental color, the sensation of red being produced by the longest and slowest of the visible light-rays. This color always typifies the active use of power. It relates primarily to the physical body, but also has a vitalizing effect on the finer spiritual body. It correlates with alchemical Sulphur.

In the color red, there is a connotation of the primitive, or of the basic beginnings, such as the Hebrew 'Adamah' red color of the ground. (Adam means 'red earth.') The red man first dwelt in America. Man evolves from lower red through the succeeding colors to the highest violet in the color scale. The root word for red is "reudh" the same as for ruby and means 'ruddy, red.'

Red is exciting. It burns fiercely with a fiery warmth and with power. It symbolizes the externalization of a thing on any plane. As the first ray of manifested being, it is called the Life-ray, or the life-giving principle of creation, and is of a positive and magnetic vibration, projecting life, strength and vitality. Red vitalizes all living matter, giving energy, strength, courage and activity. Its influence is hot and dry, and tends to incite action.

It stands for passion and sentiment, as well as the extrovert or practical realist - active, genial and vigorous. It is essentially a physical color, the essence of energy, associated with the element Fire and the planet Mars. As the color of the blood, it is sometimes connotated with brave and heroic deeds in battle, or with sublimation. Such surging and tearing passions as love, hatred, courage, or revenge are intensified by this ray, and an overbalance of red rouses temper, harshness and a streak of cruelty. It may cause a tendency to allow animal passions and desires to rule the judgment, or to manifest obstinacy and inconsideration.

Psychologically, it has much to do with desires and impulses brought over from earlier states of personal unfoldment. Certain red vibrations act upon the subconscious mind to arouse primary instincts of desire-nature. The physical power also inspires the more heroic qualities such as courage, love, adventure, enthusiasm, and the pioneer spirit. It represents the pulsation of blood, and animal life.

The Red cosmic ray is found at the thermal, or heat end of the spectrum. Thus its nature is warming and stimulating. Red is the warmest color and it is the color which, used in room decorations seems to appear closer than it really is. Rooms decorated with soft red tone are more stimulating to brain workers than those furnished predominantly with cold blue. However, caution is advised not to overuse red, for too much of it is disturbing and overtaxing, tending to make one irritable or nervous. A small dash of red can give an energizing uplift. Properly used it increases vigor - seeing red, call to action, banner of life and freedom, excitement.

Red has little effect on the intellectual centers of the brain. When red is seen in the aura it reveals such qualities as ambition, leadership, sociability, or generosity. The fulfillment of its influence is seen in men of action, of courage and optimism. They are likely to have strong love natures, more on the physical level, or the plane of the senses and emotions, less responsive to the mind and reasoning faculties. Persons who strongly manifest this ray dislike being dictated to, and excel where they can lead or supervise. They have power to do things, or to move others. They are prominent in movements of a pioneering nature, because this force is forward-looking, but destructive to systems of limitation, or to false knowledge.

Red is the first visible color in the spectrum with a wavelength of one 37,000ths of an inch. Under the red vibration we find many destructive forces such as war, sensual red-light districts, anger or fear. A man can never be made to fight until he "sees red." It is a color both irritating and aggressive. In nature, heat associates itself with red. Fire is red. In emotions people turn red with passion, embarrassment, or anger. Selling is found easier with the use of red vibrations. High pressure salesmanship is predominantly red. Products for sale sell faster and easier on red shelves or with red in back of them than other colors. The decorations of many restaurants are red because it stimulates the appetite.

Red looks warm, and is much used in cold weather to provide a cheering note. People sometimes use red to lift the morale or to attract attention. Red can be worn when it is desired to warm any part of the body, and for cold feet red tissue paper placed inside the stockings will have a more warming effect than the coarser heat of a hot water bottle. Red flannel underwear is much warmer than the same weight of white or other shades of color.

Varying shades indicate different qualities, bright clear tones being preferable to murky ones. Heavy shades usually are preferred by domineering, arrogant persons of a sensual nature. Dark red indicates deep passions of whatever kind. Snapping and sparkling red is emitted in violent passion. Animal energies including amativeness or sexual love put out a most beautiful grade of red.

Dark cloudy red shows cruelty. Reddish-brown shows sensual, voluptuous nature. The best shade to cultivate is rose red, the symbol of universal love. Dull sensuous pink signifies the reproductive urge. Clear shell-pink means creative love. Soft salmon-pink means universal love for all humanity. The creative urge of music, sculpture and poetry.

Red signifies the Holy Spirit, or the Love of God, sometimes also martyrdom. Red signifies power and fire, blood and sublimation, charity and active love. It is associated with emotions, love and hate. Among the Romans it meant sovereign power. The Cardinals dress in red. It is the color ascribed to St. John, and the martyred saints. It signifies love of action, and was used during Pentecost to denote the Holy Spirit.

Red in Foods & Chemistry

Red foods are best given along with red treatments, such as cayenne pepper (Capsicum), cloves, musk, balsam of Peru, tomatoes, beets (roots and tops), radishes, red cabbage, watercress, spinach, eggplant, most red skinned fruit (plums and apples), red cherries and red berries. Correct diet is of great importance in color healing, partaking of the foods with the analogous coloring. The fruit and vegetables build while animal sources produce toxic conditions. Use cayenne pepper in soups, salads, and various drinks such as tomato juice and lemonade. It supplies extra energy and pep, but use it sparingly as it may burn the colon. It is anti-inflammatory in the digestive tract and stomach.

Drugs with red are bromine, capsicum, iron, red cedar and musk. Oxygen develops the red principle in the blood. Red light, like red drugs, is the warming element of sunlight. Ether (C_4H_6O) and alcohol (C_2H_6O) in which the ruling element is hydrogen is bright red in the spectroscope. Also ammonia and potassium are spoken of by physicians as being arterial stimulants, rubefacient, and raising the pulse. Red and orange lights increase plant growth.

Red is radiated from 6 metals: iron, zinc, copper, rubidium, titanium, and bismuth. It is also radiated from potassium, ferric oxide, ferrous-tri-oxide, ammonium carbonate, bromine, slaked lime, hydrogen, and various alkalines. Glass used for red color treatments should contain some of the above minerals.

THE COLOR RED IN TREATMENT

Red is active in the motors centers of the brain and works in every muscle, both voluntary and involuntary. It controls the glandular center in the body connected with the sex organs. Red stimulates the adrenals and arterial blood, and exercises much influence on the health and vitality of the body. Red rays cause reaction to occur, resulting in the release of adrenalin into the bloodstream. Red light increases the amount of hemoglobin in the blood, and improves circulation by raising body temperature.

It is the natural antidote for blue-cold conditions, which it counteracts. There is an inorganic iron inside the body that is activated through the Mars center. Red applies in cases of blood disorders impaired vitality, depletion, defective circulation, depression, fear and worry. It stimulates the liver and the various senses, particularly the sense of sight. The red vibration affects the head above the brows, the eyes, and the brain as a source of motor impulses affecting muscular activity of the body. It is responsible for breaking down cell structure, as does each move or muscular action.

Red controls the subtle center at the base of the spine, the coccygeal chakra, which controls the ductless gland that releases adrenalin. Red light stimulates this center and causes hemoglobin corpuscles to multiply in the blood, raising the body's temperature and liberating energy and dispersing mucous forming diseases. (But this use of red must be used with caution.) A person who is neurasthenic and generally run down will be quickly brightened by being put in red surroundings. Care must be exercised not to over-stimulate, and the red should be changed as recovery takes place.

Red helps to stop dizziness and stimulates bowel action. It insulates against cold and increases the blood pressure. Red heats the body and increases circulation. It has a releasing and expanding principle overcoming inertia and contraction. It helps to stimulate vital and metabolic functions animating the skin and glands. Red is helpful in eruptive fevers in bringing the eruptions to the surface. It brings fresh blood to the parts upon which it is focused and clears congestion. It has been used for the treatment of smallpox, shortening the course of the disease and preventing pock marks. Also indicated for small pox, scarlet fever and measles, relieving congestion of vital organs.

Red tones up the whole nervous system. Tuberculosis patients are benefited and made to feel energized under red light, but depressed and enervated under blue and other colors. Used on the feet, red rays improve nerve function. The tone to use is a rich deep geranium or vermillion with a slight wash of carmine. It is often called Signal Red and this is the hue that has the strongest thermal properties and the longest wavelengths of the visible spectrum.

Red can be beneficially used in cases of neuralgia, rheumatic conditions, deep-seated congestions of internal organs and consumption. Other uses of red are indicated in paralysis, blood aliments, colds, lassitude, melancholy. Red is not to be used with patients who are excitable, emotional or nervous, but it should be used where there is a lack of vitality in the system. Also it is to be used where emaciation is noticeable, where hands and feet assume a blue cast in cold weather, or where there is deficient nutrition, a dormant condition or with cold inflammations.

People benefited most from the red treatments are the anemic and subdued type of neurotic. Red haired persons, those who are full blooded or who drink too much alcohol become overly irritated under red light. Extreme debility will be diminished by short treatments, but in most conditions red is to be avoided.

Red is not advisable with a naturally inflammatory condition, florid countenance, red hair, feverish, excitable temperament. With insane asylum patients, red rooms made them much worse, but they became quieter in blue surroundings. Red should seldom be employed without using other rays - too much may cause dangerous fevers. It should only be employed where immediate action is necessary. Use it only a few minutes at a time, then use blue, or place wet bandages about the head. Usually it is best to hold a blue glass over the head and the red glass over the rest of the body.

It should be used primarily as a local application. When modified to pink, it can be used instead of orange on an emotional patient. It can be irritating to the eyes and increases an inflammatory condition.

Red is a Liver Energizer - an Irritant, a Vesicant, a Pustulant, a Rubefacient, a Caustic and a Hemoglobin Builder. It is also a Sensory Stimulant.

Successful Treatments in Red Light

A boy of eight, attacked by paraplegia and almost completely paralyzed, was covered with a white sheet, and given strong red baths for one or two hours. In three weeks he walked firmly and entirely recovered in two months.

Consumption in the third stage, both lungs involved, in a woman of thirty-five, was relieved by red baths in about two weeks. In two and a half months she had entirely recovered.

Nervous prostration and complete exhaustion suffered by a man of forty-five was remarkably helped by the first red ray bath which acted as a tonic upon both mind and body. Small doses were given at first and increased gradually. In three weeks he was completely recovered, and continued to attend his business throughout that time.

A woman of forty-five, delicate from birth, completely overcome by any exertion, became bedfast during the change of life. The blue and red light treatment was applied, alternated according to variations in her condition. She recovered rapidly and remained in better health than ever before.

Color Variation

Ruby is a deep red, like carmine. It should contain neither yellow nor violet. Two glasses of manganese-violet and copper-ruby may have to be super-imposed.

Ruby stimulates vitality and the flow of the life stream, acting as a general tonic without any particular effect on the nervous system. It increases resistance and stimulates metabolic action and the production of hemoglobin. Ruby activates the stomach, liver, pancreas, kidneys and spleen. It decreases circulation especially of the venous blood but does not raise the temperature much. Like violet, it destroys parasites and bacteria.
Ruby light color contains an exquisite element of iron as well as other enkindling substances, which animate the blood. It is good for a dormant stomach, but in the case of irritation, violet is better. For very acute irritation, blue is best. As a wash, ruby is good for rousing the skin when inactive.

It is indicated in all cases of tuberculosis and anemia, provided that the anemia is not caused by syphilis. If in doubt as to the color to use in treating disease, use ruby. It covers the greatest field owing to its penetration and stimulation. It relieves gastric troubles. For cancer, it should be alternated with short exposures of green to produce a vital rhythm.

Ruby is a very mild antiseptic. It helps one overcome the desire for drink or drugs. It clears the blood through stimulation. Related to the feet and toes. It denotes turning in toward manifestation, but on a higher note.

Ruby balances the emotions giving relief to all phases of these unbalances. It is indicated in nervous conditions accompanied by melancholia or grief, and in sexual neuroses. With its recuperative Green complementary, it is of great benefit. As with green, use this for all disorders regardless of their names. It makes it possible for other colors to be more effective. It balances the sexual desires of both sexes.

Ruby will produce similar stimulating and depressive effects as those of both scarlet and violet but it works a little more slowly. If one does not know whether it is high or low blood pressure, magenta raises or lowers it automatically as is needed. It stimulates or depresses the arteries and veins. It gives all kinds of changes for heart conditions regardless of the names. Nothing can give relief to the heart with such rapidity and accuracy, as does ruby. Use this primarily on the areas around the heart and kidneys.

Ruby is an Auric Builder, Cardiac Energizer, Diuretic, Emotional Stabilizer and Suprarenal Stimulant.

THE COLOR ORANGE

Orange is the second fundamental color vibration, a hot and dry color, but less intense than red. It can be made by a combination of red and yellow, the color of flames. The heat rays of orange are therapeutically more powerful in heating than red, as they exclude the coloring rays of the active blue-violet end of the spectrum. The orange ray is linked with the vital force that flows into the body from the Sun, and is thus highly valuable. It is concerned with the task of absorbing and distributing vital energy.

Orange, in fact, is the symbol of energy, physically revitalizing and acts as an antidote to feelings of repression and limitation. It calls forth self-confidence and positive thinking, and thus has value in such fields as salesmanship and display.

Orange combines the physical energy of red with the mental qualities of yellow and has a releasing effect on both. It aids assimilation, distribution and circulation, not only of bodily substances but of ideas and mental concepts. Orange, therefore, is of vital importance mentally in the assimilation and visualization of ideas. It also has the effect of conferring optimism and courage to the mind, with the will to succeed.

Orange is warming, cheering, non-electric and non-astringent. In normal, well-developed expression, the orange vibration makes for strong vital health conditions. By reflex upon the consciousness, it manifests in an aspiring, frank, magnanimous, generous, humane, firm and honorable disposition. It can sometimes indicate pride in murky shades.

Orange indicates thought translated into action, there to become the realm of instinct and habit. It is definitely a plus vibration, and care should be exercised in its use, since it could lead to overstimulation. Some people cannot harmonize with the orange vibration and therefore should not wear it. Used in excess, it inclines to feverish trouble, domineering temperament, inordinate ambition, fondness of display, overindulgence and prodigal wastefulness of vitality and resources. Therefore, this color must be used with discrimination according to the individual's nature. Its strong vibration can be modified with one of less potency, such as blue, yellow, or green.

It is through the center corresponding to the orange ray that the cosmic Life-energy enters the personal field. This color is also harmonious with the Sun and with the metal gold. It is also connected with the absorption of subtle forms of energy from the atmosphere, and with the utilization of these in the higher intellectual functions. The Orange ray influences the process of digestion and assimilation.

The Orange ray is one of the best of the yellow group. It is the color of vitality and mental force, and relates to wisdom. Combining the vigor and stimulation with the gaiety and gladdening qualities of yellow, it symbolizes magnanimous warmth and prosperity, plenty, harvest, autumn, glory, kindliness and expansion.

Orange in the Aura

Bright, clear orange indicates the tonic force of health and vitality.
Excess of Orange denotes vital, dynamic force.
Deep Orange indicates pride.
Muddy, cloudy Orange indicates a low intellect.

Orange in Foods & Chemistry

In drugs, emetics are yellow with some Red and Orange, such as Indian Hemp, Lobelia, Tartar Emetic, Bloodroot, acting principally on the pneumogastric nerve. Laxatives and purgatives have yellow as the chief color, with red in drastic purgatives. Some foods include may apple, senna, Colocynth, laxative fruits such as figs, prunes, and peaches.

Metals and chemicals which radiate Orange include selenium, iron, nickel, calcium, rubidium, manganese, carbon, oxygen (slightly), and many alkalines. The glass to use in Orange color treatment should contain selenium, uranium oxides, manganese and red lead.

Foods with the Orange color include the orange skinned vegetables, and fruits such as carrots, rutabagas, pumpkin, oranges, apricots, persimmons, mangoes, cantaloupes, tangerines, and peaches. Include such orange foods to help build strong lungs. There is also a rumor that the moderate use of spices can be helpful to the lungs, acting as well as mild laxatives and stimulants to the digestive tract. Since we are also warned against an excess of spices, be cautious to use them lightly, because most spices come under the orange color influence.

THE COLOR ORANGE IN TREATMENT

Orange or deep amber combines red and yellow, which can usually be used in its place. It is especially useful for warming and animating cold, negative and dormant conditions. It can rouse and vitalize chronic inflammation before this is treated with blue or green, and is beneficial for a cold cervix. In eruptions such as smallpox or scarlet fever, it is useful to alternate with blue so as to produce a vital rhythm. Orange is stimulating and animating to both blood and nerves. Yellow is the central principle of nerve and brain stimulus, with the more violent types of stimulus tending toward the red or orange.

Orange affords quick recuperation from fatigue produced by mental work. Orange affects the hands, arms and shoulders, the lungs and the upper ribs. It is a powerful tonic, with a direct effect in building the energy of the body, and has some influence on the emotional or astral nature of man. Orange can also be used to treat the spleen, kidneys, bronchial tubes and chest conditions generally. It is useful with venous disability.

Orange is to be avoided in fevers, acute inflammation, delirium, diarrhea, neuralgia, palpitation of the heart and with any overexcitement, yellow or orange reddish tones are not to be used. Lack of the orange vibration, on the other hand, or interference with its free expression, causes health to suffer and depression of both physical and mental reflexes.

Orange stimulates and increases the pulse rate, but does not affect the blood pressure. It strengthens the etheric body, enlivens the emotions and creates a general sense of well-being and cheerfulness. If used for too long at a time, it will over-stimulate and result in tiredness.

Orange is indicated in all cancerous or malignant growth conditions. In the precancerous stage, orange will often abort the oncoming illness. In all cases where malignancy is suspected, orange is indicated with its complementary violet.

It may be used successfully to relieve menstrual cramps and limited discharge. It relieves spastic and sluggish colon and the small intestines. It increases all kinds of discharges and eliminations. Boils are helped by using orange to draw various conditions to a head, such as carbuncles, boils and abscesses. The congestions can then very easily be activated by the yellow color to be discharged by the body.

Orange in treatment is a Respiratory Stimulant, Parathyroid Depressant, Thyroid Energizer, Antispasmodic, Antiarchitic, Emetic, Carminative, Stomachic, Aromatic, Lung Builder, and Galactogogue.

Successful Treatments in Orange Light

Chronic asthma is treated by taking half a glass of Orange solarized water warmed in the Sun, every ten minutes for an hour while the Orange light is focused on the chest and throat. The treatment should be repeated every three to four hours until relief is felt. During healthy intervals oranges should be eaten freely, or an ounce of orange solarized water taken between meals.

Blue light can be applied to the throat after the chronic symptoms are removed in order to strengthen the health of the larynx. In the early stages of asthma, blue-indigo water and light are often helpful.

Prolapses: The patient lies with legs and feet raised to a 45 degree angle and the orange light is directed at the knees toward the trunk. The patient is asked to breathe the orange color upward, feeling the consciousness and bodily functions including circulation moving upwards. This treatment should be given twice daily until the organs adjust themselves.

Gallstones can be dissolved by breathing in the peachy universal love rays, the divine solvent, drinking the orange radiated water and applying the orange light.

Bronchitis if chronic may take some months to improve as the orange color has to first rectify stomach and bowel disability.

A case of gallstones combined with rheumatism in the legs was successfully treated by having the patient relax face downwards on the couch and the healer sweeping the hands downward from the hollow of the back over the legs and feet eliminating the trouble. The orange light was then focused on the feet for ten minutes, and twenty minutes spent in raising the light up the back of the legs to the lumbar vertebra, where it was held for fifteen minutes on the chakra at the spleen. A magnetic treatment with the hands was given at this point in a circular outward movement.

The patient had six treatments after which medical x-rays showed the gallstones were gone and the rheumatic pains had ceased. A recurrence of the trouble may occur, however, unless the emotional bitterness and resentment that has caused the crystallization of the stones is removed entirely from the mental-emotional nature. The universal color affirmation and visualization is powerful in doing this.

Inflammation of the Kidneys has been cured by orange light treatment using the light and taking the orange solarized water, in one case a large quantity of gravel being passed in three days and no subsequent pain.

Costiveness (constipation) Sunlight was applied through a yellow-orange glass focused through a lens on the bowel. In ten minutes perspiration was produced over the whole body and in ten minutes a gentle passage occurred without pain.

Anemia treated by focusing orange light on the spleen for thirty minutes.

A wet cough with much phlegm is greatly helped by the orange light treatment upon the lungs and the orange colored water taken internally. Two treatments in the morning and one in the evening will generally bring about improvement in two weeks.

Color Variation

Yellow-Orange is an intermediate color which in the Orient means renunciation. It is a very mild stimulant, its cheering influence assists in overcoming the blues, worry, or mental depression. It has to do with the chest and mammary glands, the stomach, the diaphragm, lower lobes of the lungs, and upper lobes of the liver. It helps promote digestive functions and assimilation.

Yellow with some orange and red excites the nervous system in drugs of light. It is animating to the nerves, being laxative, diuretic, stimulating to the brain and liver. It is especially desirable in constipated, paralytic and stupid conditions. It should not be used in delirium or diarrhea.

THE COLOR YELLOW

Yellow represents the third color vibration. It is called one of the rays of mind, stimulating the mental faculties in the creation of thought, and giving help in visualization. It is most active in the higher brain, or cerebrum, as its general organ of expression.

Yellow comes from the root word "ghel" which means 'to shine.' Yellow is the color of religion or veneration. St. Peter is sometimes depicted robed in yellow. A pure Yellow represents revealed Truth.

It poses opposite meanings: of the Sun and divinity on the one hand, or when murky, it relates to Judas' deceit and treachery. Yellow is the medium color or the center of luminosity.

Generally it arouses optimism, cheerfulness, and a balanced outlook on life, equilibrating in its effect. Yellow aids in developing tact, mental alertness and discrimination, and helps to establish emotional balance. It is said to make joyful through greater attainment of the soul and one's Self, and suggests as well the joy, merriment, comfort and cheerfulness of the fireside.

Heroes and heroines of older legends were usually depicted with yellow hair, as it seemed to suggest the lighter or finer side of life. Yellow to many of the ancients was the animating principle of life. To the Chinese, it symbolizes nobility. Being active on the mental plane, yellow is called the wisdom ray, related to the astral or mental consciousness. Its rulership of mind and high intellect indicate a love of mental employments and pleasures, rather than physical. Yellow relates to science and usually appeals to person of intelligence and discernment.

Both astrologically and alchemically, the yellow vibration corresponds to Mercury, and to the metal quicksilver. It aids in the alchemical process having to do with extracting materials for body structure. It is sometimes used to symbolize illumination, dissemination, magnanimity, or intuition.

As the ray of maximum light, yellow holds first place in the spectrum of brightness and luminosity. It has a positive magnetic vibration, with a powerful effect on the nervous system, although in healing work when nerves are very active and irritable, yellow should not be used. The yellow ray of mind, flashing as it does, golden streams of awakening light, can be used for mental stimulation. It is a good color for writers, artists, and all creative workers - the paler shades being especially inspirational. A yellow shaded light is helpful when doing mental work as in studying. Too bright a yellow, however, while stimulating at first, will soon have a somnolent effect.

A murky yellow is associated with sickness, treason, deception and cowardice, from which the expressions came "yellow streak," "yellow journalism" etc. It is also used as a symbol of quarantine. Excess of yellow leads to indecision and a tendency to substitute thinking and talking for action. Its deficiency may result in over-activity if red and orange are strong, or in mental depression if blue is preponderant.

The red, orange, and yellow rays are magnetic in effect, flowing upward from the earth toward the solar plexus. Rudolph Steiner says "Yellow must shine outwards, it wants to radiate. When yellow is given weight, it loses the luster of spirit and becomes the color of gold. If it is to become fixed, it must become mineralized - color fixed in matter." Father Paul said, "Yellow has an influence that is vitalizing and refining. Yellow is the purging Light of Christ. Gold comes out of the whole thing."

The opposite color of yellow is violet. It is the yellow factor that denotes richness in milk or cream - the butterfat content, rich in Vitamins A and D. The right shade of yellow can produce a sensation of sunlight and warmth, but a slight change can make one feel nauseous. Airlines no longer use it because certain shades encourage more frequent cases of motion sickness. Yellow foods should be avoided during air or sea voyages.

Yellow is excellent where 'food for thought' is needed. Grade school student's grades rose when yellow was applied to the walls of the classroom. Yellow enhances life and gives a feeling of joyousness and cheerfulness. Yellow is a stimulant of the mental faculties and is useful in cases of mental lethargy or deficiency. As a mental color, it stimulates the nerves, and invigorates. It relates to the powers of intellectual analysis and concentration, and acts on the brain center of the nervous system. It also stimulates the psychological functions, and when used with complementary violet, gives a feeling of passive contentment.

Gold symbolizes the Sun, the state of glory, the solar rays and currents. Gold present in the aura is very good. Golden yellow indicates the intellect in its higher phases and aspects, and high soul qualities.

Yellow in the Aura

Dark, dingy yellow indicates jealousy and suspicion.
Dark yellow signifies deceit and treachery.
Dark, mustard colors show unpractical people, somewhat lacking in character, who dream away the idle hours.
Dull, lifeless yellow indicates false optimism, visionary mentality.
Pale, primrose yellow means great intellectual powers.

Yellow in Foods & Chemistry

Such yellow substances are saffron, valerian, mustard, dandelion, senna, podophyllum (may apple), colocynth, sulphur, figs, gluten, castor oil (yellowish), ginger. All purgatives or laxatives stimulate the nerves of the bowels by means of the yellow as the leading color. In drastic purgatives, as well as in emetics, diuretics and brain stimulants, a good deal of the red substance is also used as a blood rousing principle.

THE COLOR YELLOW IN TREATMENT

In healing, Yellow is active in the region of the upper intestines, in the shoulders, arms, hands and lungs. Through stimulation of the higher and finer functions of the brain, it aids in the development of mental alertness. It also has an effect on the heart, the dorsal region of the spine, the spinal cord, and the aorta. It has some affinity with the liver and intestines, with a cleansing and healing effect on the skin. Both sensory and motor nerves are stimulated by yellow, especially the solar plexus. It can be used in all negative, despondent and melancholy conditions.

It acts as a purgative and laxative when the colon and abdomen are exposed to its rays. It stimulates the liver and gall bladder assisting in the sufficient supply of bile in the colon for better elimination. Constipation is greatly relieved by drinking solarized water. Charged solid substances with yellow appear to have a similar effect.

It is generally inadvisable to use yellow in nervous or excitable conditions, in insomnia, nausea, diarrhea, heated or inflammatory fevers, or nerve troubles such as sciatica or neuritis. However, a short exposure to the yellow alternated with a full exposure to its complementary blue may be useful in establishing a vital rhythm.

Yellow is well-advised in all hepatic and gastrointestinal cases. The yellow or amber of the deep therapy bulbs is a cholagogue or hepatic stimulant. It acts directly upon the solar plexus and stimulates peristaltic movement. It is doubtless the most exquisite laxative in the world, as tested for many years. A prominent New York manufacturer declared it was worth thousands of dollars to him and a lady whose whole being was revolutionized by it called it the 'elixir of life.'

Yellow solarized water can be charged in a few minutes of bright sunshine, or by placing yellow-orange lenses out of doors where light can strike them constantly. Put fresh water every two or three days to keep it fresh. In severe cases, it is well to take two to four teaspoons of charged water before each meal until the bowels move, or even every hour if needed. For constipation, homeopathic doses of yellow solarized water and yellow light focused in the navel for thirty minutes night and morning will remedy the condition and should be accompanied by the yellow deep breathing. If the effect proves laxative, a does of blue solarized water will counteract it.

Yellow, because of its sodium principle, is used most successfully in cases of ulcers to build the stomach, and relieves stomach trouble generally. It increases the appetite and aids in the assimilation of proper food for better nutrition. The lymphatic glands are affected by food assimilation and are activated by yellow.

Yellow is used as a stimulant for a sluggish liver when the bowels are not in good order. Exposure to yellow should be brief. For all kinds of paralysis, chronic rheumatism, dropsy and other dormant it is beneficial. It has a stimulating effect on cells and activity of the skin without causing much rise in temperature. It is used most successfully in cases of paralytic strokes and nervous breakdowns and deficiencies. Infantile paralysis responds rapidly to the yellow irradiation. It assists in loosening calcium and lime deposits such as arthritis, neuritis and similar conditions.

This color also increases metabolism, and activates all body functions except the spleen. An overactive spleen is depressed by yellow. The use of yellow for diabetes stimulates the pancreas for better assimilation of natural starches and sugars. Yellow is useful in tuberculosis, counteracting the vibrational rate of this affliction, but it requires somewhat prolonged treatment.

Yellow helps in the stimulation of eyes and ears.
Yellow assists in ridding the body of worms.
Yellow stimulates the heart for better circulation.
It is a capital for cerebral stimulation and an emetic and laxative.

Yellow is an Alimentary Tract Energizer, anthelmintic, Cathartic, Cholagogue, Digestant, Lymphatic Activator, Motor Stimulant, Nerve Builder, and Splenic Depressant.

Successful Treatments in Yellow Light

A <u>Chronic bronchial</u> irritation was treated with hot sunlight filtered through yellow glass and was immediately relieved.

<u>Costiveness (constipation)</u> was relieved by drinking half an ounce of water in an amber colored vial held close to the yellow rays of a kerosene lamp for seven minutes. A patient using yellow solarized water found it an unfailing cathartic and exhilarating to the spirits.

<u>Dyspepsia</u> may come either from an increase of red or blue in the system. The increase of red is usually indicated by excessive thinness, the increase of blue by over-weight. In treating either, the yellow color breathing should be done early in the morning and half a glass of yellow solarized water taken between meals. The yellow light should be focused on the solar plexus daily for thirty minutes. There should be improvement in about a week.

If the patient is overly thin, showing an increase of red, indigo treatments should also be given. The light and water should be given twice daily for a month or two.

<u>Paralysis</u> in some cases can be benefitted by use of the yellow ray as this is primarily a disease of the nerves, brain and the lack of power in ordering the nerve force to act.

Diabetes originates from poor digestion and more fat formed than blood. The same treatment as for dyspepsia will benefit this condition, with the yellow ray and yellow colored water given twice daily, decreasing the formation and increasing the blood. Two months will be required.

Color Variation

LEMON loosens and dissolves calcium and lime deposits throughout the body as does yellow, but in a slightly different manner. Use lemon for all chronic disorders as these conditions must be loosened and dissolved before they can be eliminated from the body. Lemon color loosens colds and like yellow, it also stimulates and builds the brain for clearer and more positive thinking. If this treatment is followed by yellow, better results can be obtained.

This color activates the thymus gland for more rapid growth in retarded children, and is most effective as a bone builder in cases of breaks or soft bones. The lemon fruit is the best known fruit to loosen and clean. That is why it is so helpful in cleansing diets.

Lemon color is an Antacid, antiscorbic, bone builder, cerebral stimulant, chronic alterative, expectorant, laxative and thymus activator.

YELLOW-GREEN is an intermediary color between yellow and green in the spectrum. It is a slightly depressant color, it quiets the nerves, correcting the tendency to overconfidence. It quickly relieves headache caused by autointoxication or unequal blood pressure. It is related to the small intestine upper part of the large intestine, to the pancreas and spleen, to the lower lobes of the liver.

THE COLOR GREEN

Green is the fourth fundamental color, the central column of the shining spectrum of color. It occupies the point of balance in the solar spectrum midway between the thermal (heat) end, and the cold (electric) blue end of the spectrum. Thus it becomes the color of harmony, and the ray of balance and concord.

Green is the color of Nature, and the keynote of our planet Earth. Man's first environment was a garden. The green radiance is essential to our health and happiness. Certain mystics speak of it as the ray that counterbalances cause and effect. It emits calm, refreshing emanations of peace and harmony. Green is also the connecting link between the black of mineral life, and the red of animal life. In terms of epoch, that of the green ray is midway between the lower periods of struggle and bitter experience, and the higher periods of soul growth and spiritual faculties.

As a combination of the yellow/wisdom and the blue/truth rays, Green opens and enlightens the mind and spirit with wisdom and truth. The color is rich in the emerald Life-prana, the inexhaustible energy of nature. Green inspires harmony and peace on the inner or subjective plane and attracts success and progress on the outer or objective plane, along with abundance, evolution and supply.

The fulfillment or completion of the subjective aspect of Green is a balanced mind, kindness, peace and harmony, sympathy, adaptation, and generosity. The Life of Christ shows many of the beautiful qualities and emanations of the green ray. As the color of nature and vegetation, it has a soothing, harmonious radiation that is essential for the well-being of our nerves, and the proper functioning of our bodies. Green pastures and fresh air are indeed a wonderful aid in recuperation of health, and it seems in line with this that the leaves of the Tree of Life are used for healing. As a color of earthly, perceptible growing things, it represents the field of sensation, and also the victory of life over death, as in spring. It represents fertility of the fields, immediate natural life.

It is a blend of feeling and thought - the color of self-revelation and growth. We vibrate to green when we become conscious of motive, and test ourselves, often to our dissatisfaction. Green is the color of youth, the springtime of the year when vegetation shows its greatest growth and vigor. It brings resurrection, new life, hope, peace, mature expressing power. Variations in green bring different vibrations, meditation, liberty, and adventure.

The root word for Green is "ghre" which means to 'grow' or to become green. Green light gives us the energy of the Sun in its safest and most natural form, and is identical with the green plant energy known as chlorophyll, which is prescribed by medical science specific for the heart. Green in any form is one of the finest tonics for the red nerves. The shade or chroma should be bright and clear, but much will depend on individual preferences.

Green is the symbol for charity. It is refreshing and cool, suggesting youth, peace, and relaxation. The expression "green horn" indicates the youth and inexperience associated with green. When green is darkened with black it indicates envy, jealousy, and superstition. "Green with envy" is the recognition of this. "Green around the gills" is another expression indicating an upset condition, an approaching illness, the result of fear, or a case of biliousness.

Desolation, poverty, lack and auto suggestion are relieved by the green ray. It impels imagination, keeps the creative sap of life flowing. Freely functioning, this color vibration makes for grace and symmetry in physical action and form. It enhances artistic ability and stimulates creative imagination. When strong it lends good taste, love of beauty, and fondness of pleasure and the lighter enjoyments. It is the color of the planet Venus.

Green In Religious & Church Symbolism

Green garb relates to vegetation and spring, and the immediate or natural life - growth and sensation. It also represents triumph of life over death, as spring over winter. In pagan initiation rites it symbolizes water. St. John is sometimes shown in green, for spiritual initiation. It also reflects the Epiphany season, the visitation of the Magi and initiation rites in the life of Christ. It denotes hope, regeneration and immortality.

Green in the Aura

Green is the symbol of Harmony and sympathy, the Higher Mental Plane. Bright, clear rays bespeak good qualities.

Clear Green - sympathy.
Jade Green - tact and diplomacy
Light Green indicates prosperity and success.
Mid-Green shows adaptability and versatility.
Excess of green in the aura denotes individualism, supply, and independence. Dark green shows deceit.
Grayish Green shows deceit or duplicity.
Olive Green shows treachery, double nature.
Soft Green of indescribable Beauty means benevolence

Use the Green ray for mental restfulness, or emerald green for mental revitalization, and higher emotions, such as compassion and sympathy. As a mildly sedative and depressant color, green promotes physical relaxation necessary for brainworkers, and is beneficial for the subconscious activities involved in invention and artistic creation.

It gives poise in action. Green conveys a feeling of life and tranquility.

THE COLOR GREEN IN TREATMENT

Green has a double action, animating the nerves and cooling the blood. Green vitalizes and restores the blood and nerves with nature's magnetism. The green vibration heals heart disorders, emotional complexes, and soothes the nerves of the head. A calm green light is an excellent remedy for headaches. A weakness or deficiency of green vibration causes physical centers to function badly and the related emotional excess, sensation seeking, and waste of time in mere amusement.

It is beneficial to absorb as much green as possible by using green lamps, green clothing, green decorations in the house, and by eating green vegetables. Chlorophyll, the green in plant food is most beneficial. It is sometimes called the cleansing principle. Foods containing green coloring include most of the green vegetables, and fruits, which are neither too acid nor alkaline in their reaction. Green is neither heating nor astringent, neither acidic nor alkaline. Green prevents fermentation. In therapy it both soothes and exhilarates.

Without the green ray we feel desolate, and the loss of vitality. Green is the color of balanced strength, progress in mind and body. It stimulates the heart center and affects the blood pressure by energizing the brain through the yellow in it, but moderates the pressure through the blue. It acts as a tonic to both mind and body and strengthens the spirit. All sensitive, nervous people need the green ray. It has a purifying effect on the blood, better than drugs.

The Green used in healing should have neither a blue nor a yellow tint but should be the clear emerald green. The particular tone of green to be used depends upon the pulse rate and tension. A low tension requires a lesser intensity of color and a high tension a greater intensity. Green is most effectively used alternatively with other colors and as a rhythmic or corrective with ruby and red.

Green is an aphrodisiac, a pituitary stimulant, a disinfectant, a purificatory, an antiseptic, a germicide, a bactericide, a detergent and a muscles and tissue builder. Green is calming on the mentality and the nerves, as well as on the physiological functions, is anti-inflammatory and soothing to the stomach and liver. It reduces blood pressure by acting upon the sympathetic nervous system relieving the tension of the blood vessels and thereby lowering the blood pressure. The dilating of the capillaries produces the sensation of warmth.

Green decreases vital and metabolic action, being helpful in the treatment of jaundice and biliousness. It is useful in calming nervous, excitable, and irritable people, and in hysteria. Green acts upon the nervous system as a sedative and is helpful in sleeplessness, exhaustion, and nervous irritability. With nervous disorders it will work very well without reaction. It is good with neuralgia and shell shock. It is emotionally soothing and it loosens and equalizes etheric body.

Some diseases aided by green are ulcers, cancer, syphilis, influenza, erysipelas, colds and boils. It is not to be used where there is anemia or lack of vitality. Green is called a negative color but can sometimes be used where blue is beneficial. Much like blue, green is cooling, though the yellow part of green gives some nerve stimulus good for uterine inflammation. The green may often be used to advantage over the small of the back and lower spine in cases of over-sexual warmth and seminal emissions.

The metals and chemicals radiating green are sodium, copper, nickel, chromium, cobalt, platinum, aluminum, titanium, carbon, nitrogen, ferrous sulfate, sulfate, hydrochloric acid and chlorophyll. Glass to use contains combinations of the above chemicals plus iron oxide. The nitrogen or protein principle of the green builds the muscles and tissues. The best form of protein is always obtained from green live foods from the vegetable and seed source. Animal proteins are toxic and destructive when used in large quantity, not conducive to creative living.

Many elements needed by the body are picked up from the air as it enters the lungs. It is universally recognized that oxygen and some hydrogen are taken from the air but few realize that nitrogen is also taken from the air and used for building through the protein principle. This is one of the many important reasons why smoking is so bad. It prevents the lungs from properly absorbing and using these elements or gases. Heavy smokers find that they have cravings for toxic animal proteins because they become deficient otherwise. Plants obtain a great percentage of their nitrogen from the air also.

One therapist called Green the master color because it affects and stimulates the master Pituitary Gland for better control of other glands and organs throughout the body. The green dissolves blood clots thus preventing stoppages in the head, heart, and legs. Green is the basic color for all disorders of either chronic or acute variations. Start schedules of irradiations with one or more green exposures. This makes the other colors more effective. Many cases may be cleared up with the green alone. If you find it difficult to determine whether conditions are acute or chronic, use green and you will be right.

Green builds muscles, tissues and cells; many masses of hardened and crystallized congestions are broken up and eliminated this way. This includes cancerous and tumorous conditions. Green affects the throat area, thyroid, parathyroid glands, kidneys, adrenals and the vasomotor system. Green aids the skin in its function as an organ of elimination and relating to the sense of touch, the lumbar region of the spine, and an area just above the pelvis.

Since germs and virus exist only in toxic waste matter, green is marvelous as an eliminator of such conditions. Its use on open sores and decaying flesh is truly wonderful.

Successful Treatments in Green Light

<u>Low Blood Pressure</u>: Focus the green light over the heart for half an hour treatments and drink the green solarized water at hourly intervals between meals in half a glass dosages. Eat freely of green salads.

<u>High Blood Pressure</u>: Follow the same treatment but use a paler green.

<u>Neuralgic Headaches</u>: Relieved by just looking at the green light. Sitting in green light for an hour at a time will refresh exhausted nerves and aid in optimistic thinking. If the headaches come from insomnia and lack of rest indigo -violet will help.

<u>Erysipelas</u>: Can be treated with blue alternated with green. Green is indicated in all hepatic derangements and all ailments that are caused by hepatic or portal conditions. For reconstruction and recuperation, green is a wonder. If treated immediately, before going too deep, is healed by the green ray treatment.

<u>Cancer</u>: This can originate through a perversion of the love force in cruelty during the present or a previous life and its cure requires a change of feeling. The universal and then the green breathing affirmations should be used, followed by green solarized water taken internally and the green light focused over the location of the cancer. The green ray applied through a compress of yellow silk soaked in brine has been used successfully in the treatment of malignant growths as it gives forth a highly refined radioactivity on the etheric body.

<u>Syphilis</u>: Another perversion of love, yields to green water and to green light treatment.

<u>Ulcers</u>: Can be relieved by the green ray given over a long period of time. As they are caused by fear, anger, criticism and antagonism, the opposite of these emotions built in through the use of compassionate green will heal them.

<u>Influenza</u>: Requires both the green and blue light, as do mucous fevers, whooping cough and croup.

<u>Colds</u>: Colds of the head yield to green water and green light, sometimes with the help of indigo. Boils, Gumboils, whooping cough, dysentery, and cholera all yield to green water and light treatments. For boils, use a green compress if possible. For gumboils gargle frequently with green water. Boils are helped by indigo light drawing out the pus and green light helping healthy flesh to form over the wound.

Green with its complementary red tones up the system after a debilitating disease such as the flu. After all fevers green can be used advantageously. It is very useful in stimulating the sex glands and will be found to be helpful to men and women.

THE COLOR TURQUOISE

Using turquoise for skin building gives immediate relief and correction from sunburn, hot liquid burns and severe skin injuries. Some of the most severe destruction of the skin has responded and healed rapidly without even leaving a scar. For areas where the skin, flesh and tissues are destroyed, alternate turquoise with green.

Various infections and all kinds of fevers respond to turquoise. It gives fast relief from poisons causing fatigue. These poisons are produced by work, play and exercise as the cells and tissues are broken down making them tired. Use turquoise at any time to correct this. It also gives relief from insomnia.

Blue-green (turquoise) is a sedative and depressant, its action is expressed through the nerves and muscles of the voluntary nervous system. It is beneficial for an overactive and over stimulated brain. It depresses an overactive thymus gland. It relieves various kinds of irritation and itching. It is very cooling and relaxing. This applies especially for headaches and many kinds of extreme pressure or swelling conditions.

Turquoise is an acute alterative, cerebral depressant, skin builder and tonic.

By arousing the activity of its opposite color, it can be used to treat the throat area. In general, it relates to the genito-urinary organs, the urethra, the prostate gland, and the descending colon and rectum. Blue and green together aid in digestion.

THE COLOR BLUE

The word BLUE comes from the root "bhel" meaning to "shine," "fire," "lash," "burn," and "white."

Blue is the fifth fundamental color vibration, and is both symbolically and medically the opposite of red in its effects. Blue is the color of Spirit, or of the higher mental or spiritual body. It is the color from which the highest inspiration is born. Not for the coarse material-minded, it is for the ethereal, spiritual natures.

As the night sky, "Blue is darkness made visible." The darker hues, when clear, especially denote refinement and higher thought. In spiritual symbolism, Blue is the color of the sky, and suggests the unveiling of Truth, as the heavens with clouds pulled back. It also represents heaven and heavenly love. It suggests prayer as an ascending scale of blue light or aspiration with stars flying upward. Blue is the traditional color used in the church to represent the Virgin. From Rudolph Steiner, "Blue is the lustre of the Soul."

Blue is called the coldest color, and when used in decorations makes things seem farther away. Blue as experienced through the senses draws the individual out to a larger world. It gives the feeling of immensity, transcending the small and petty. When mixed with white, it has a gentle uplifting effect, withdrawing us from the material. Blue is helpful in short sight as it draws the vision outwards. It deflects the forces of the head downwards. Some hospitals have found that patients recover more quickly if they are placed in blue rooms following major surgery. Sometimes blue is used for quieting violent inmates of mental hospitals. Blue can be an emotional sedative.

Blue stands for the vertical, as with height and depth; blue sky above, blue sea below. It is also used to symbolize heaven, Truth and Eternity. The ancients spoke of the blue sky as that which "endures forever." It is the first color belonging to the cold, non-stimulating or astringent division of the spectrum, its effect being to slow down and steady the energy of the reds and yellows. It is considered a color of calmness, courtesy, harmony, and happiness. Psychologically, the blue vibration raises the consciousness to the realm of spirit hence its value in spiritual healing, meditation, and devotional services.

Father Paul states: "Blue has a fine, soothing, electrical effect. Blue is the color of renunciation."

The Cosmic Soul, or higher mind of nature expresses much of the peace, beauty, and harmony of creation through the Blue and Green rays. The blue has a calming effect on mind and nerves, and is successfully employed in cases of insomnia. Rudolph Steiner states that using a dark blue lamp by the bedside will help induce sleep. Truth, peace, poise and serenity are the main features of the mental influence of the Blue ray. It has to do with the gateway of the spiritual aspect in man, and with his religious instinct, or his devotional and mystical nature. It is related to the spiritual body, and thus the root cause of your present condition of life.

Blue clear water or endless space is relaxing, quieting to the emotions. It has a carefree feeling. But dull blue, or too much blue, can feel drab and depressing. One with "the blues" needs a warmer color to cheer him, in the reds and yellows. Ice blue is very cold. A room without sun might feel colder if it were painted blue, but a sunny exposure would be relaxing in blues or greens.

"True Blue" describes the person who is loyal, devoted and sincere, someone to be trusted. In its highest brightest sense, it is a happy and uplifting color, like the "bluebird of happiness." It is a color of virtue, also of illusion and mystery, according to the hue. Whereas a red dress might suggest allure and audacity, one would incline to look up to or respect a woman wearing blue.

From a psychological standpoint, blue is a spiritual and meditative color. It relaxes the mind and stimulates it toward spiritual and philosophical matters. The two most familiar hues of blue are the pure or cyan blue and royal blue. The cyan blue does not transmit red or ruby light. To find out if blue glass is suitable for color treatment, hold it up to an electric light bulb and see if the filaments appear pale blue or white. If they do, it is suitable. But if they appear ruby colored, the glass transmits red and is not to be used for cyan blue treatments.

The center associated with blue has to do with all bodily rhythms, such as the periods of waking and sleeping, of respiration, and even the coordinating influence of the millions of bodily cells with the connective activity which links their work together. In healing work, blue is useful for its soothing aspect, which cools the blood and quiets the nerves. It acts as a strong sedative and repressant, and is mildly antiseptic. Where pain needs to be relieved, even after treatment of another nature, blue can be used.

Darker shades reminiscent of the blue night sky are helpful for relieving insomnia. The blue vibration is also useful in matters having to do with the correction of areas such as the neck, throat, palate, larynx, tonsils, lower jaw, ears, hips, thighs, stomach, mammary glands, esophagus, upper lobes of the liver, and lower lobes of the lungs. Also the sciatic nerves, femur, ilium, coccygeal and sacral regions of the spine, iliac arteries and veins, lungs and diaphragm.

Its opposite color or complement is orange in the rainbow spectrum. Blue is the symbolic color of the element Water, and sometimes the Moon. It is also used to denote Jupiter, god of heaven, and through this influence it indicates good fortune and expansiveness. Where the blue vibration is strongly developed within a person, it inclines to make him sensitive or emotional, with a strong rhythmic sense which may express in fondness for music, dancing, or poetry. It gives a good memory, and some psychic attunement.

Where blue is deficient, poor memory may result, lack of rhythm, improper functioning of the organs mentioned above, lack of coordination of bodily cells, and/or harsh temper. Excess of the blue ray makes for over-sensitivity, uncertainty, idle visions, depressed manner, dependency on others, timidity, or digestive disturbances.

The color blue is usually associated with cold and has a cooling effect. The victim of keen frost usually has a blue skin, and snow itself has a bluish tint. Drugs which are used to allay inflammation or as astringents or nervines, are generally blue. In therapy, blue is tranquilizing, though too much is depressing. People of sanguine temperament are benefitted by blue as it cools them down, but they would be over-stimulated by red. The blue color induces sleep and relaxation from stress and strain of extreme activities.

Sometimes blue is indicated rather than red. Firmness comes from conditions of polarization - electricity, which is the blue principle. The blue of reasoning powers is a grade higher than the blue of firmness.

Blue in the Aura

Pale ethereal blue signifies devotion to a noble idea.
Pale blue indicates simplicity, innocence, and candor.
Electric Blue means great personal magnetism.
Deep blue means spirituality.
Deep clear blue signifies pure religious feeling.
Bright blue symbolizes loyalty and sincerity.

Blue in the aura generally shows a spiritual and artistic nature, with good spiritual understanding. It is the color of inspiration and devotion.

Blue in Chemistry & Foods

The metals and chemicals which radiate the blue are lead, tin, cobalt, copper, nickel, zinc, cadmium, aluminum, manganese, titanium, copper sulphate, phosphoric acid, chloroform, tannic acid and oxygen.

Foods containing the blue coloring include plums, blueberries and eggplant, etc.

THE COLOR BLUE IN TREATMENT

Blue glass for treatment should contain oxides of copper and ammonium sulphate. When a general exposure to the blue ray is given it should not last more than ten minutes and longer than this will cause a feeling of tiredness and depression. Sensitive persons feel tired and depressed if they remain in a room predominantly blue in its furnishings, though a proper soft-blue room can also bring a feeling of great peace and upliftment.

Blue is anti-inflammatory increasing the metabolic action and growth of healthy cells. It slows the action of the heart, decreases circulation, relieves inflammatory pain, lowers temperature and reduces nervous excitement, and is generally healing. Blue is not to be used if there is poor circulation, low vitality, dormant or sluggish conditions, congestion of organs, poor metabolism or cold cervix. The lowering action of blue on the nerves is not as decided as violet but it should not be used in nervous depression.

A list of the diseases which can be controlled by the blue ray include all kinds of throat troubles, fevers, typhoid, scarlet fever, chicken pox, measles, cholera, bubonic plague, apoplexy, hysteria, epilepsy, palpitation, spasms, acute rheumatism, jaundice, biliousness, colic, vomiting, purging, dysentery, diarrhea, inflammation of the eyes, bowels, skin, teeth, headaches, insomnia, nervous disorders, shock, and painful menstruation.

Blue solarized water taken internally relieves diarrhea, dysentery, and inflamed or painful stomach, gastritis, epithelial cancers, and insomnia. As a gargle held in the mouth a while, it cures beyond most remedies a cankerous or otherwise sore mouth, inflamed gums, etc.

As an eye wash for inflamed eyes it is believed unequalled. As a wash it often cures chapped hands or dandruff immediately, relieves burns, especially in the form of a compress, destroys red eruption, making the skin as soft as silk, and heals wounds and hemorrhages. As an enema it relieves inflammatory conditions of the womb or rectum very wonderfully, and is especially good when taken hot from the sun. As a nervine it is remarkable. It is not to be used wherever organs are too cold and dormant.

Blue is a cold color and causes contraction of the arteries thereby raising the blood pressure. It acts specifically on the blood and has a tonic effect, being also antiseptic and lessening suppuration.

It is beneficial in inflammation but must be used with caution if there is high blood pressure. Persons who have low blood pressure accompanied by headaches will find relief from the blue treatment, which is also beneficial in treating carcinoma. Blue causes contraction or tightening of the etheric body. It is soothing to the emotional body in cases of over-excitement and produces a marked improvement in cases of mania. In emotional conditions blue is more soothing than green. Blue is the color that has the greatest bactericidal action. It is the color to use in all acute infections and will produce some surprising results in many acute cases. Blue is relaxing to the nervous system. It is the color to use in the treatment of arteriosclerosis and cardiac hypertension.

Blue, complimentary to the ruby, is to be used for treating all cases of autointoxication, unless tuberculosis is present, in which case ruby only is to be used. All cases of syphilis are to be treated with blue. All toxic conditions not defined as to cause are to be treated with blue. Blue is a specific in the treatment of gonorrhea. It is useful in allaying the pains of cancer. It is helpful in the treatment of nervous disorders that are characterized by muscular twitching and jerking such as tics and chorea.

Blue, indigo, and violet light heal on the same principles as the drugs but with a more delicate and less harmful effect. Many case histories show the power of these colors to heal specific conditions.

Blue is an Anodyne, Antipruritic, Counter-Irritant, Demulcent, Diaphoretic, Febrifuge, Vitality Builder.

Dysentery responds readily to blue water which nature carries to the affected part internally. Care should be given the diet, avoiding meat and starches, taking sago, rice and arrowroot. Milk kept in a blue bottle and solarized for ten minutes is also good.

Colic is relieved in one hour if blue water is given every ten minutes.

Bleeding Piles respond from external applications of blue water and light. Also indicated in cases of palpitation and jaundice.

Cuts, Burns, Stings and Bruises Cuts will be healed by wet compresses of blue solarized water. When there is inflammation with the sting, then apply the blue light.

Animals respond readily to color treatment. Blue water and blue light will prevent their feeling extreme heat and are antidotes for poisoning.

Hydrophobia Bite, for man or animal, apply blue light to the wound for two or three hours daily and wash it with blue water, keeping a wet compress on it if possible. Then drink a medicine glass every three hours for the first three days, then reduce it to two or three glasses daily and later just one glass upon retiring.

Laryngitis is healed by drinking half a glass of blue water every half hour and gargling with some of it. The blue light is used on the throat.

Hoarseness is resolved by blue in small but frequent applications. At the beginning of the day use the blue breathing exercise and focus the blue light on the throat for half an hour. Three times during the morning and again in the morning use the blue breathing exercise and focus thought on the throat for half an hour. Three times during the morning and during the afternoon drink half glassfuls of blue water, gargling with some of it and holding it in the back of the throat.

Teething can be relieved by keeping the infant in the blue light for some hours every day until the heat subsides.

Goiter has been cured by focusing the blue light on the throat for half to three-quarters of an hour accompanied by gentle and etheric massage. A gargle of blue water will also help.

Fevers, which are due to the increase of red, are assisted in throwing off the poisons in the system by blue light and blue water.

Typhus responds to the blue light alone, though the blue water will also help. Typhoid can be remedied by the water alone; so can remittent and intermittent fevers but the blue light treatment can also be given with benefit.

Eruptive fevers should not have the symptoms checked while nature is throwing off the poisons and color should be used carefully, although radiated water can be given if there is great thirst.

In case of delirium, blue light may be administered.

Successful Treatments in Blue Light

Loss of Voice caused by shock was successfully treated focusing the blue light on the patient's throat for forty minutes at a time twice a day and applying violet superimposed by blue for an hour. Her voice returned in nine weeks. During this time she occupied a room with blue cellophane over the windows.

A woman of fifty-nine was afflicted with sciatica for eleven years, with knee, ankle and feet swollen to twice their normal size. Blue glass was inserted in a west window and the light applied to a large purplish lump on the ankle. In two or three hours the lump disappeared together with the pain. But subsequently swelling and pain occurred in the knee, which was relieved by a blue glass bath in less than an hour. Within a week she was able to walk easily and the useless toes of her foot became normal.

A violent case of hemorrhage of the lungs was cured by sitting at a window in which blue glass was placed over half the sash, the blue light falling on the nerves of the back of the neck for about an hour a day. After about six weeks she was much improved and red pimples appeared on her neck indicating the treatment was bringing out toxins in the blood.

A month old child had a hard tumor on the sub maxillary region that disappeared in forty days under an hour's daily treatment under blue glass. Had the light been concentrated on the place through a lens and alternated with yellow and red, the cure would have taken place more quickly.

Healing Power of Blue and White Sunlight

Blue and white in combination are more animating than blue or violet light alone as it contains the electrical power of the blue and the healing power of all the rays in the white light. Since the blue color has a chemical affinity for red, the blue rays of light seize upon and combine with the red portion of the white light. This will produce a greater heat than the white light alone if more white than blue is used. But if an equal amount of white and blue glass is placed side by side, the effect will be much more cooling than the transparent glass alone.

Blue and white combined give the penetrating, calming principle of blue and the warming, animating principle of white light, enabling both to be taken at the same time, one part of the body being under the blue color and the colder parts under the clear glass. In fever or nervous conditions more of the blue should be used; in chronic cold, glass of pure sunlight should be used almost solely.

Associated sun and blue light applied to the bare spine and hip of a vigorous young man suffering from rheumatism of the sciatic nerve brought about a healing in three weeks, after all the usual medical and galvanic treatments had failed.

Blue glass placed in the upper part of a sunny window affected the cure of a woman's long-standing invalidism and nervousness. She sat in the blue sunlight and clear sunlight continuously, letting the blue rays fall directly on the spine for about twenty to thirty minutes at a time, morning and afternoon. The change in two or four weeks was very noticeable, the color returning to her face, her appetite becoming better and strength returning and vitality returning. In about six weeks she was able to go up and down stairs and before long to walk out doors.

THE COLOR OF INDIGO

Indigo, also called blue-violet, is the Sixth fundamental color, denoting intuition and spiritual perception. As a symbol of the Mystic Borderland, it has to do with spiritual attainment and self-mastery, wisdom and saintliness. It lies between the blue and the violet in the spectrum, the name comes from the Greek "Indikon" which is a blue-violet dye obtained from various plants of the genus Indigofera. The chemical compound contained in this dye is $C_{16}H_{10}N_2O_2$.

Indigo is stimulating and regenerating to mind and soul, and is one of the rays of the future race-consciousness, extending the inner vision and opening up new fields of comprehension and knowledge. This is the vibration on a parallel to a power in us, which knows when, and how to put on the brakes. The mental effects of its usual activity are concentration, poise, and deliberation, suggested by the expression "indigo mood." In religious symbolism, indigo represents metaphysical thought.

Its deficiency might indicate eccentricity or rashness of behavior, aimless dreaming, or weakening of the bony structure. Too much indigo tends to increase fearfulness and caution, or poisons caused by retention of waste in the body. This color in its relation to the lower end of the spine has to do with functions that excrete waste from the body. It has a cooling and purifying effect, and is used as an astringent or antiseptic. It is a slightly stimulating color, containing a little red. It can halt tissue degeneration, and clear skin, or be used for the clean healing of skin eruptions or wounds.

It is a safe neutral anesthetic, its anesthetic effect brought about by causing a hypnotic condition in which the patient is insensitive to pain while fully conscious. It has been used in successful treatment of mental disorders, obsessions, nervous disorders, insomnia, and matters having to do with the eyes, ears and nose. Also it is used as an antidote to frustrations, to fear complexes or general negative conditions, by taking action on personality and character.

It has effect on the organs of sight, hearing and smelling, on the nervous, mental and psychic faculties. It corresponds to the areas of the knees and skin, bony structure of the skeleton, the kidneys, the sweat glands, lumbar region of the spine, the vaso-motor system, the excretory system and the sacral plexus. Indigo has some relation to the transmission of life. Its planet is Saturn and its metal is lead.

Blue, indigo or violet substances as aconite, ergot, indigo, the galls, sulphate of copper (blue vitriol), together with a moderate form of the acids, which have the blue principle of oxygen in them (including sulphuric, phosphorus and nitric acid) are spoken of as being refrigerant astringent, antiseptic, arresting hemorrhage, narcotic, and allaying spasms.

Chloroform ($CHCl_3$) has the blue-green, blue, indigo and violet strong in its spectrum, and is called a direct sedative to the nervous system. Tannic acid, though bluish yellow externally, has strong oxygen, and its blue and indigo principle seems to be potentized by the hydrogen in a way to make the substance as a whole, highly astringent. Aconite, whose flowers are a dark violet blue, is called a powerful nerve sedative and anodyne. Opium, which has the red and yellow elements in predominance and yet being called a narcotic, and sometimes an astringent, may be thought to convert the principle, but it should be remembered that opium is a narcotic by overexciting and congesting the brain, and is an astringent in part by drawing the vitalizing ethers from the bowels to the head, which thus leaves the bowels weak.

Minerals and chemicals radiating indigo are chromium, iron, copper, strontium, titanium, potassium, bromide, cupro diamonium sulphate, chloral hydrate and oxygen. Indigo foods partake of both blue and violet coloring. Glass for indigo

110

treatments should have cupro diamonium sulphate, which is used in mazarine glass.

Drugs used for healing have the blue coloring and include aconite, belladonna, foxglove, ergot, cranesbill, logwood, blackberry, and nitric acid.

The blue, indigo and violet being cooling and contracting are nervine astringent, refrigerant, antiseptic, febrifuge, anti-inflammatory, narcotic and anti-spasmodic. They are not to be used in cold, bluish and chronic conditions, unless considerable excitability is present.

Blue is as pronounced in reducing nervous excitement as red is in producing it, and may be administered in small doses as a general sedative, creating a disposition to sleep. But as soon as sleep begins the bath should cease. In ordinary cases the blue bath should be about two hours through a window containing alternate blue and plain glass. This may be longer than most persons can endure comfortably unless the head is protected.

THE COLOR INDIGO IN TREATMENT

Indigo gives relief from swellings and extreme acute pain. It gives a sedative effect. Use Indigo for an over-active thyroid gland and for stimulation of the parathyroid for better and freer breathing. It can be applied to the nerves of the cranium, stomach, bowels and kidneys. It is indicated in conditions of delirium, emesis, diarrhea and diuresis occurring through overheating. With diarrhea a blue glass can be placed over the bowels or blue charged water can be taken by the tablespoonful. A case which had lasted five weeks was stopped in two days by a patient taking a tablespoon of water two or three times a day of the solarized indigo water. After the first day or two she took only an occasional sip of the water and was entirely healed.

By reflex action of its complementary color, yellow-orange, it can be used to aid in difficulties relating to stomach, breasts or digestion.

Successful Treatments in Indigo Light

The sense of smell can be restored by use of the peachy pink breathing affirmation combined with imagining the aroma of delightful flowers. Then a little indigo water is to be sniffed up the nose several times a day and a little gargled in the back of the nose. A compress of indigo silk wet with indigo water is to be placed over the nose and indigo light radiated through it, while the patient inhales deeply and uses the indigo color breathing affirmation.

Bleeding of the nose can be stopped by snuffing and bathing the nose in indigo water, then focusing indigo light on the nostrils. One with frequent nosebleeds will be benefitted by a dose of indigo water at bedtime for a week. Indigo is also helpful to relieve internal bleeding.

Indigo is indicated in cases of facial paralysis, lung troubles, pneumonia, bronchitis, bronchial croup, whooping cough, asthma, phthisis, mental ills, delirium tremens and insanity. Pneumonia responds best to indigo light unless there is hemorrhage, where blue light should be used. Dry cough can be stopped by drinking indigo water.

Infantile paralysis is healed by indigo light and water.

Dyspepsia yields well to the same.

Indigo is an astringent, hemostatic, pain reliever, phagocyte builder, respiratory depressant, sedative and a thyroid depressant.

Inflammation occurring in the parts of the body for which indigo color treatment is indicated should first have the heat reduced by using the blue, then apply the indigo to bring about better functioning. Eyes inflamed from digestive troubles will be helped by using blue glasses and then having indigo light turned on the face.

Granular Eyelids and chronic ulcerated corneas, styes, and bloodshot eyes require the same treatment, blue light and indigo light with indigo water that generally affects a cure in a few weeks.

One of the eye afflictions successfully treated with the indigo ray is Cataract. This can come from an adamant attitude toward persons or conditions. One case of this was treated psychologically first asking the patient to do the universal breathing exercise and giving her a salmon pink rose to meditate upon, suggesting that she use this color in her room furnishings. Before the treatment was begun, the room was flooded with soft pink light to help dissolve the harshness of the patient's mentality. Indigo breathing was then practiced while both eyes were bathed with indigo radiated water and wet compresses of it put on the eyelids and forehead. After this the indigo light was radiated on the eyes and forehead and the patient was asked to inhale more deeply. The light treatment was continued for thirty minutes and the forehead etherically massaged with the fingertips, the healer visualizing the indigo light flowing through them. The patient was given a transparent indigo eyeshade and asked to sit in the sunshine whenever possible with the indigo light directly on the eyes.

A case of encroaching blindness due to shock in which there was no organic eye trouble was remedied by changing the colors of the patient's room furnishings from orange and yellow to green, and violet light treatments were given twice a day. Partial recovery occurred in seven weeks and in seven months the sight was nearly normal.

Deafness, which can come from a mental attitude of unwillingness to hear certain things, as well as from physical causes, can be relieved by use of the peachy pink light and affirmation and bathing the face and ears with indigo water every morning. Then the indigo light is to be used on the ear.

Earache inflammation can be reduced by blue light and if there is a pimple or discharge from the ear, a gentle syringe with blue water, followed by indigo light and indigo water. Abnormal sounds in the ears, if they come from too much heat in the brain, will be stopped by indigo light on the head with the feet kept warm and the bowels open.

Pulmonary diseases are caused by fear and the eradication of fear is therefore essential for a permanent cure. The power of consciousness is directly keyed to the blue rate of vibration and this can be fixed by drawing the blue light of poise and serenity and then color breathing in the blue ray. A long-standing case needs to be disinfected with the deeper blue of indigo light, which the atomic impurities during the bombardment of atoms may be cast out. The entire atomic structure of the body is

114

caused to split up and multiply by the bombardment of cosmic forces. This process is stimulated by color and within it is the remedy for complete healing. Much of the rebirth of cells goes on within the blue-indigo light for the atoms of the body do not die but are split up into new substances and new activities.

Anesthesia can be produced in the safest form known to science through the use of the indigo light. The indigo raises the consciousness of the patient to such a high rate of vibration that he becomes unaware of happenings to the physical body having withdrawn his consciousness to higher levels. This is not at all the same as hypnosis.

A six month old child who had been in convulsions for four hours was given up as dying when a half grain of milks sugar that had been exposed too the violet and blue rays was administered. In some fifteen minutes the convulsions stopped and the child recovered completely.

Creeping Palsy due to a mental helplessness is relieved by having the patient concentrate on the word "serenity," then putting him under the blue light moving it down the right side and up the left. (The direction is important). Deep green light is next focused on the soles of the feet and slowly moved up the spine. Indigo light is now radiated on the throat center for twenty minutes and then moved down the right side and up the left, stopping for ten minutes to focus the light on the soles of the feet. Before going to bed a warm bath should be given while the indigo light is over the tub and then a rub down with indigo cloths. If a tub bath is not feasible, the bath can be given on a rubber sheet on the bed using a warmed blanket to prevent chilling. Salt bags solarized with indigo, as previously described, can be used in place of a washcloth. The indigo should be kept shining over the bed. If the patient does not respond immediately to the treatment, the indigo light can be left shining during the night, but this is only an extreme measure.

Experiments were made with milk of sugar, placing some of it in red and yellow rays of the solar spectrum and some in the blue and violet rays. After some time of such exposure, the taste of the former to a sensitive was tepid and nauseous, but that of the latter was cool and refreshing, confirming the properties of these colors as previously shown.

THE COLOR VIOLET

The symbol of spirituality is the highest color vibration of the spectrum, vibrating at 790,000,000 vibrations per second. Violet is the seventh or final principal color of the rainbow spectrum, manifesting in many hues such as heliotrope, amethyst, orchid, royal purple, wisteria and lavender, each of a different significance. All other rays are likewise subdivided into various hues. The major divisions of the Violet ray are related to the earth plane as its most material aspect, and Amethyst, the more spiritual aspect of this color.

The Violet ray vitalizes the spiritual nature with life-giving power and animates and expands the soul-consciousness. It is of a positive magnetic vibration, but not physical. The soul which lacked this ray totally would be barren and dry. This is not a color for the masses, but appeals more to sensitive and soul-conscious types who seek spiritual unfoldment and enlightenment. It inspires the highest ideals, as for example great works of art, music and poetry. It stimulates the desire to benefit humanity, and in its perfect fulfillment the Violet ray is manifest in the prophet, the mystic, the seer or inspired teacher, the great poet or musician.

Violet is the spiritual color - its purest ray being amethyst. It is the "Voice in the Silence" - the inner eye which is the bliss of solitude. It is the individual matter of meditation - prose cannot adequately describe poetry. Violet is a mixture of feeling and action, and is the spiral's turn where the highest does service to the lowest. Its rays are shortest and closest to the Light. Amethyst is the ray of spiritual Mastery. It borders the ultraviolet, also a part of the Violet ray, and is the purest vibration we can see. In contrast to red, which deals the physical body primarily, amethyst influences his highest spiritual nature. The ultraviolet rays are more rapid and potent in effect.

Violet carries the highest vibration of visible light, with strong electrochemical properties, and its rays are stimulating to the nervous system, inspiring to the mind, arousing the soul qualities of mysticism, spiritual intuition, and idealism. There is some relation of the color Violet to the abdominal brain with its record of the history of the cosmos, also to nostalgic memories. The deep Violet rays are very stimulating to the nervous system, inspiring, purifying, nourishing those cells in the upper brain that expand the understanding and idealism.

The Violet ray in normal balance gives fondness for outdoor life, lending soundness to all bodily functions. Psychologically, there manifests a love of ceremony, of charity, and interest in established forms of religion, good manners, respect for law and order, and a generally reasonable and conservative attitude toward life.

Violet is a powerful healing agent, with a direct influence on the brain and nerves. It is stimulating to the spiritual nature, and a strong purifying force. It is used to stimulate the spiritual body, to treat mental, nervous, and cerebral troubles. It is used for relaxation, to restore mental equilibrium and cure lack of poise caused by the rush and bustle of modern life, so difficult for sensitive people. Its use for a short time each evening is found especially valuable for brain workers, helping considerably to ensure restful sleep. This use also aids in the development of spiritual consciousness, the clairvoyant and psychic faculties, and is of great value in meditation and concentration.

One of the greatest investigators of the science of color, Leonardo da Vinci, the painter, said that the power of meditation can be ten times greater under violet light falling through the stained glass windows of a quiet church. Wagner had violet hangings about him when he composed his lofty music. The Comte Saint Germain healed the sick with violet rays and removed blemishes from gems with it. Violet in the church is used for penitence.

Deficiency in this ray may affect health through poor circulation or impure blood. Psychologically there would be expressed the opposite of the normal mental qualities indicated above. Overbalance, or too much of this ray in an individual may manifest as pompous, materialistic, a stickler for details of convention, form and ceremony - a rigidly conservative type.

In religious symbolism, violet stands for love, truth, passion and suffering. It also represents idealism and sublimity. Violet represents penitence, sometimes sorrow. It is also a color of royalty, formerly worn by those of royal, imperial or high rank. It is the color symbolizing not only power, but service and devotion to the people.

Amethyst combines the stimulation of red with the tonic of blue and is a particularly vital color. It should be used sparingly.

Violet, combining the red and blue colors, symbolizes rulership, dignity, richness and majesty, the color of royalty. On the less materialistic side it refers to the passion of sorrow, to meditation, aspiration, seclusion, reverence and upliftment. Violet is often called the power ray associated with kings and it is the ruler of the kingdom of the body and all its parts. Its planet is Jupiter, and its alchemical metal is tin.

Lavender which is violet tinted with white symbolizes spirituality and sweetness, dainty and soothing.

Violet in the Aura

Violet indicates spirituality.
Deep violet stands for high spiritual attainment and holy love, the Divine Redeemer.
Pale Lilac and Wisteria tints represent Cosmic Consciousness and love for humanity.
Bluish Violet represents transcendent idealism.

Violet in Foods & Chemistry

Foods having violet coloring are eggplant, purple broccoli, beet tops, purple grapes and blackberries, along with purple cabbage. Metals and chemicals radiating violet are manganese, barium, iron, rubidium, aluminum, calcium, cobalt, strontium, titanium, silver chloride, and arsenic. Violet glass for color treatment should contain manganese and cobalt.

THE COLOR VIOLET IN TREATMENT

Violet is similar in its action to blue but more cooling and depressing to the mind and nervous system. It can produce lethargy, melancholy and deep relaxing sleep. It is a powerful bactericide and parasiticide, effective in the treatment of ringworm, itching and similar infections with pus. It increases the red corpuscles. Violet is useful in all pulmonary ailments. Its chief effect is upon the nervous system and it is not to be used in cases of melancholia, depression, sleep sickness, paralysis, rheumatism, gout, low vitality or any cold, negative conditions of the system.

Yellow used alternatively with violet produces a strong vital rhythm. It is complementary to yellow which is used for tubercular conditions, and benefits phthisis by increasing the resistance of the tissues. Violet relieves over-stimulated nerves, and acts as a depressant for violent mental conditions. It reduces excitement and extreme irritations. There is a close correspondence between areas affected by the blue and violet vibrations. Both are active in stomach, mammary glands, and liver.

Violet is mildly stimulating, antiseptic, and regulative, which promotes the normal flow of fluids throughout the body, and relieves congestion of the nerve currents. It is useful as an antiseptic when applied to delicate membranes, such as the eyes, or the mucous membranes of the mouth, nose and genito-urinary organs.

It refers to the ankles, the legs between the knees and ankles, to the digestive system of the sympathetic nervous system, and the epigastric ganglion. It relates to the sacral regions of the spine, the sciatic nerves, the femur, hips, and thighs, feet and toes.

Diseases which are aided by violet include nervous and mental disorders, neurosis, neuralgia, sciatica, epilepsy, cerebrospinal meningitis, cramps, concussions, tumors, kidney and bladder troubles, and diseases of the scalp. Violet stimulates the venous blood and purifies it. It affects not only the blood vessels, but also the heart and lungs. Violet depresses all overactive conditions of the organs and glands. However, there is one exception, violet builds the white corpuscles and stimulates the spleen.

Violet made by the radiation of ruby and its complementary blue, can be used in treating all conditions caused by active gonorrhea. It is useful in all renal deficiencies.

The violet combines the blood-warming red and the cooling antiseptic blue. It is excellent for the lungs, stomach and kidneys and other parts where animation without irritation is needed. Red-violet is good for a dormant stomach, but blue-violet or blue is best if the stomach is hot and excitable. Violet charged water is especially good to help digestion if taken internally, is excellent as an enema in leucorrhea and ulcerated uterine organs or rectum. It makes a good nasal douche for catarrh.

As a fine wash for baldness and dandruff, it should be rubbed in over the whole head from the end of fingers repeatedly wet in it.

Violet lowers the blood pressure to give relief from many headaches and pressure pains. It relieves toothache. Violet depresses the over-active kidneys and adrenal glands. Due to its hypnotic effect, one finds restful and relaxed sleep using violet. Violet gives similar relief from pain and suffering as narcotics give, without the harmful after effects.

Violet is found to be most effective in giving relief to all types of fever. It may be used interchangeably with turquoise wherever indicated. Violet helps reduce sexual desires and over-emotional disorders.

Violet is a cardiac depressant, leucocyte builder, lymphatic depressant, motor depressant, and splenic stimulant. Violet is a heart and arterial depressant, analgesic, anaphrodisiac, antimalarial, antipyretic, hypnotic, narcotic, renal depressant, sex builder, and vasodilator.

THE COLOR WHITE

White is the arch transmuter embracing all the colors and lifting the powers of any one of them to their utmost perfection. But it can only be used in its spiritualizing sense. The visualization for the in breathing of the white light requires the stilling of every restless thought and feeling a profound calm encompassing the consciousness. White is not a color ray in the healing sense although it magnifies the power of each, but its appreciable activity operates on the higher planes.

Its power manifests everywhere. It is the white Light of Christ consciousness which produces the healings at such places as Lourdes and other shrines. All color is an aspect of Light. The spectrum in proper proportions produces White. The white light without filters combines all rays. Thus we have made full circle. White light appears in all minerals and chemicals though most strongly present in platinum, silver and quartz. Silver in religious symbolism, represents the Moon, and the lunar currents in the nervous system. Lenses to use in healing with the white light are best made of quartz. White light consists of course in the sunlight, which has been used in healing down through the ages. It is recognized as an antiseptic and a caustic.

The purity of a color will have its counterpart in the purity of its symbolic meaning. Thus primary colors will correspond to primary emotions (such as those of children) while secondary or more subtle colors express meanings of further complexity.

White is the color produced by reflection of all the rays of the Solar spectrum, and it is from White Light that all color radiates. White multiplies and projects the properties and powers of Light. Everywhere accepted as the symbol of goodness and purity, it also indicates holiness, pardon, and innocence of the soul. When used for religious habits, it signifies innocence of soul, purity and holiness of life.

White light is both the synthesis and the negation of color. Any color can be diluted with white almost to the extent of obliterating it. In like manner the grosser elements of man can be visualized as being gradually transformed into finer and finer essences through the spiritual power of white light. White light can only be used imaginatively by the effort of visualization, picturing it for instance, as a fountain of water with the sun sparkling on it, or a beam of radiant light shining down producing a unifying and harmonizing effect.

White is stimulating to those who respond to its high rate of vibration. It is the end product of color. There are many variations of white - dead white, bone white, snow white, pearl white, and foam white. It speaks of virginity, purity, peace and holiness. As a color of Light itself, it represents Illumination, Ascension, and Revelation.

The visualization of White light in connection with respiration has had interesting results in conducted experiments. Patients are asked to visualize the colors of the spectrum in their order from red to violet. The red increases the respiration in the upper part of the chest, the green affects the epigastric expansion, the violet produces deep abdominal breathing. If the response to the various colors is normal, the breathing will be smooth and regular from the upper part of the chest downward. If the patient fails to respond to any one of the colors, the breathing will become jerky or irregular as the color is visualized. But when contemplating white, such as white flowers, or a snowfield, the breathing will be fuller and deeper than when thinking of any of the colors.

While breathing deeply feel yourself lifting the power and energy within you to meet the descending white light, and see it multiplying and surrounding you in a white wall of protection. If you are the healer, place the patient in the center of this all-encompassing white light, and then extend it to include all in the world.

The affirmation for the White Light:

> A dazzling white, pure ray serene, uplift my soul to meet
> thy gleam;
> Fill every atom with power supreme, make ill-thought
> life seem but a dream.
> O resplendent Father, seven rays in One,
> Teach me to blaze my hidden Sun,
> Love merged with strength, no more diverse,
> Encompass the mighty universe.

WHITE = WILL

The great power of light is shown by the transformations it is ever making in mineral, vegetable and animal forms, and colors. A copper wire held by such a sensitive in a dark room and the other end attached to a metal plate in a ray of sunlight registered immediately on the sensitive as an icy cold principle, so cold as to stiffen the hand. From this it was deduced the finer elements of sunlight are cold.

Water standing in the sunlight for five minutes produced a pepper-like burning when the sensitive drank it, when standing for twenty minutes in the sunshine it was powerfully magnetized.

THE COLORS GRAY, BLACK & BROWN

Gray

Gray is the "impartial reflector" because it looks almost white when it is the brightest color around and almost black when it is the darkest color around. It looks grayer only when both lighter and darker colors are present. It is a comparison function made by the brain unconsciously. It is a color between white and black, having no definite hue, ash-colored, technically of an achromatic color. It is defined as any color with zero chroma from white to black.

Any two lights of exactly opposite color unite to produce white light, but two pigmentary colors, being opaque in nature, when mixed with direct opposites produce gray. For this reason, gray is said to be the symbol representing the perfect blending or neutralization of any two pairs of opposites.

There are many tones of gray, each with its own significance. The color of ashes, it has been used to portray humility, inertia, or indifference; neutralization, depression or sadness; death of the body and immortality of the spirit. In Mystery teachings, as the union of opposites, it represents Wisdom.

Black

Black negates and absorbs the powers of light. Having no brightness or color, reflecting no light, in absorbing, it "takes" rather than gives light, and thus symbolizes the opposite factors, the absence of light, or darkness. Some of its symbols are matter, fermentation, putrefaction, occultation, ignorance, and penitence. Mineral life, fertilized land, germination in darkness, prime matter, and the mystery of the Unknown. Black means "without brightness or color." Black and White, when used in religious habits signifies humility and purity of life.

Brown

Brown is the color of earth, a dark color combining red, yellow and black. From an external or negative standpoint, brown signifies worldly status, materialism and sometimes decay. Golden brown indicates worldly pleasures. Dark dingy brown signifies greed and miserliness. Muddy brown is earthiness. Dull brown is selfishness. Golden brown is conservation. Clear, pleasing shades of brown are warm and comfortable to the eye, with a feeling of friendliness. Brown used in religious habit signifies renunciation of the world.

PSYCHOLOGICAL & PHYSICAL SYMPTOMS BY COLOR

Red

Improves circulation
Stimulates Adrenal Glands
Stimulates the Liver
Depression, Fear, Worry, Melancholy
Eyesight
Raises body temperature
Dispels Mucus
Stops dizziness
Stimulates the bowels
Brings eruptions to the surface
Tones the whole system
Removes congestion
Tuberculosis, Anemia, gastric troubles, consumption
Paralysis, blood diseases, colds
Rheumatism, neuralgia, measles, smallpox

Orange

Stimulates blood and nerves
Quick recuperation from fatigue
Flushes out inflammation
Good for the cervix
Powerful tonic
Increases the pulse, does not effect blood pressure
Enlivens emotions
Strengthens the aura
Creates cheerfulness and sense of well-being
Cancers & malignancy
Aborts pre stage of cancer
Relieves menstrual cramps and limited discharge
Relieves spastic colon
Increases all discharges and eliminations
Brings conditions to a head – boils and abscesses
Chronic asthma
Prolapses
Gallstones
Bronchitis
Constipation
Anemia
Wet cough with phlegm

Yellow

Heals nervous system
Mental stimulation
Visualization
Activates upper intestines, shoulders, arms, hands and lungs
Stimulates and cleanses liver, intestines and gall bladder
Heals skin
Aids despondency and melancholy
Purges the colon and abdomen
Relieves constipation
Relieves bronchial problems
Stimulates eyes and ears
Increases metabolism
Stimulates heart and circulation
Constipation and dyspepsia
Diabetes
Laxative

Green

Inspires harmony and peace
Relieves desolation and poverty
Stimulates creativity
Promotes relaxation and soothes
Promotes compassion and sympathy
Animates nerves and cools the blood
Prevents fermentation
Tonic to body and mind
Purifies the blood
Soothes stomach and liver
Reduces blood pressure
Treats jaundice and irritability
Calms nerves
Heals insomnia and nervousness
Stimulates the pituitary gland
Dissolves blood clots
Breaks up congestion & hardened masses
Builds muscle
Aids skin in eliminating toxins
Helps with cancers and tumors
Blood pressure – high and low
Heals headaches
Relieves ulcers
Resolves colds and fevers
Good for boils and mouth sores

Turquoise – Blue-Green

Treats sore throat
Helps genito-urinary tract ailments
Heals prostrate gland
Helps colon and rectum
Aids digestion
Anti-depressant
Good for overactive brain
Resolves itching and all irritation
Good for headaches and extreme swellings
Great for infections
Good for fatigue
Great for skin building, bruises & skin injuries

Blue

Good for teething
Relaxes the mind
Induces Sleep
Anti-inflammatory & Antiseptic
Grows healthy cells
Decreases circulation
Lowers temperature
Reduces nervous excitement
Throat troubles, fevers
Spasms & Rheumatism
Colic, vomiting, diarrhea
Inflammations of eyes, bowels, skin, teeth
Headaches
Insomnia
Painful menstruation
Canker sores, inflamed gums – as gargle
Eye wash
Cure for chapped hands & dandruff
Relieves burns and red eruptions
Inflamed womb and rectum
Tonifies the blood
Good for acute infections
Cardiac hypertension & arteriosclerosis
External – Styes, cuts, burns, bleeding piles
Laryngitis and hoarseness

Indigo

Swellings and extreme acute pain
Restores sense of smell
Nosebleeds
Facial paralysis
Lung troubles, including croup, bronchitis, pulmonary disease
Infantile paralysis
Eyes – Inflammation & cataracts
Deafness
Earache
Mental Helplessness
Related to functions which excrete waste
Slightly stimulating
Mental disorders, including obsessions, nervous disorders & insomnia
Affects knees, skin, bones and kidneys

Violet

Relieves headaches and fevers
Deep relaxing sleep
Eliminates parasites, itching and infections
Pulmonary ailments
Good for depression, rheumatism, gout & low vitality
Tuberculosis
Relieves over-stimulated nerves
Promotes normal flow of fluids in body
Relieves congestion of nervous system
Antiseptic to delicate membranes such as eyes, mouth, nose & genito-urinary
Lowers blood pressure
Sciatica, cramps, concussion, tremors
Good for kidneys, bladder and scalp
Stimulates venous blood supply, heart and lungs
Depresses all over-active conditions of organs and glands
Stimulates the spleen and builds white blood cells
Cardiac depressant, lymphatic depressant
Good for lungs, stomach, and kidneys
External – charged water is good for digestion, dandruff and baldness

PSYCHOLOGICAL SYMPTOMS BY COLOR

Red
Depression
Debility
Fear
Inertia
Lassitude
Melancholia
Nervous prostration
Neurotic, subdued type
Worry

Orange
Confidence, lack of
Costiveness
Depression
Exhaustion
Fatigue
Lack of Assimilation
Limitation
Mental debility
Negative thinking
Repression

Yellow

Costiveness
Despondency
Lethargy
Melancholia
Mental deficiency
Negative thinking
Nervous breakdown
Sadness

Green
Agitation
Biliousness
Compassion, lack of
Desolation
Excitability
Hysteria
Infertility
Irritability
Lack
Nervousness
Over-sexed
Poverty
Strain/Stress

Turquoise
Insomnia
Irritation
Over-stimulated brain

Blue
Biliousness
Coordination, lack of
Distressed
Excitability
Harsh Temper
Insomnia
Irritability
Manic
Memory, poor
Nervous excitement
Nervousness
Nervous disorders
Pain
Shock
Strain/Stress

Suffering

Indigo
Concentration, lack of
Costiveness
Day dreaming
Delirium Tremens
Fear Complexes
Frustration
Insomnia
Insanity
Mental disorders
Negativity
Nervousness
Obsessions
Rashness

Violet
Concentration, lack of
Excitement
Irritation
Over-sexed
Pain
Peace, lack of
Poise, lack of
Neurosis
Sleeping disorders
Suffering

PHYSICAL SYMPTOMS BY COLOR

Color in parenthesis also treats the same condition.

Red

Anemia
Asthma (bronchial)
Blood disorders (clots use red)
Bronchitis
Bronchitis (Orange, Indigo, Yellow)
Poor Circulation (Violet)
Cold Feet
Colds (Lemon, Green, Indigo, Orange)
Congestion of Internal Organs
Consumption (Indigo)
Constipation (Yellow)
Dizziness
Dormancy (Orange, Yellow)
Enervation
Eruptive Fevers
Feeling Run Down
Impaired Vitality
Loss of Blood Corpuscles
Malnutrition
Measles (Blue)
Mucous (Lemon, Green)
Neurasthenia
Neuralgia (Green, Violet)
Paralysis (Yellow)
Paraplegia
Pneumonia (Indigo)
Rheumatic Conditions
Scarlet Fever (Orange, Blue)
Small pox (Orange)
Tuberculosis (Ruby, Yellow, Violet)

Ruby (Red Variation)

Anemia (as long as syphilis is not present)
Arthritis
Asthma (chronic use orange)
Bacteria (infection)
Congestion (Green)
Crystallized Deposits
Dispels the Fetus
Hair
Kidneys (Orange, Green, Indigo, Violet)
Liver (Yellow, Green, Violet, Upper Lobes- Blue)
Lumbago
Menstrual Pains (Blue)
Nails
Pancreas (Yellow)
Parasites (Violet)
Pigmentation
Plethora
Sinus Troubles
Skin (Green)
Stomach (Green, Blue, Indigo, Violet, Troubles – Yellow)
Stomach – Inactive, Dormant
Tuberculosis (Red, Yellow, Violet)

Orange

Arms
Absesses
Asthma (chronic)
Boils (also Green)
Breast Milk, brings in
Bronchitis (Red, Indigo, Yellow)
Carbuncles
Chest Conditions
Chronic Inflammation
Cold Cervix
Colds (Lemon, Green, Indigo, Red)
Colon Troubles
Cough, Wet
Dormancy (Red, Yellow)
Epilepsy (Violet)
Flatulence (Gas)
Gall Stones
Gout (Indigo)
Hands (Yellow)
Inflamed Kidneys
Kidneys (Scarlet, Green, Indigo, Violet)
Malignant Growths
Menstrual Cramps
Menstruation, cessation of
Phlegmatic Fevers
Prolapse
Rheumatic Conditions, Chronic (Chronic - Yellow, Acute - Blue)
Rickets
Scarlet Fever (Red, Blue)
Shoulders (Yellow)
Small Intestinal Difficulties
Small pox (Red)
Spleen

Yellow

Acidity
Aorta
Arms
Arthritis (Scarlet)
Bronchitis (Orange, Red, Indigo)
Calcium (Lime) Deposits
Colds (Green, Indigo, Orange, Red)
Colon Troubles
Congestion in Colon
Constipation (Red)
Diabetes
Dormancy (Red, Orange)
Dropsy
Dyspepsia (Indigo)
Ears (Blue, Indigo)
Eyes (Indigo)
Gall Bladder
Gastro-Intestinal Trouble
Hands (Orange)
Heart (Violet, Green)
Hepatitis
Infantile Paralysis
Liver (Scarlet, Green, Violet, Upper Lobes- Blue)
Lungs (Violet, Indigo, Upper Lobe- Blue)
Low White Blood Corpuscle Count (Violet)
Lymphatic Ailments (Violet)
Mucous (Red, Green)
Neuritis
Pancreas (Scarlet)
Paralysis (Red)
Rheumatic Conditions, Chronic (Chronic – Orange, Acute - Blue)
Scurvy
Soft Bones
Shoulders (Orange)
Spinal Cord
Spine
Stomach Troubles

Strokes
Thymus Gland Troubles
Tuberculosis (Red, Ruby, Violet)
Ulcers (Green)
Weak bones (Indigo)
Worms

Green

Adrenal Glands (if overactive, then Violet)
Blood clots
High Blood Pressure/Hypertension (also Violet, cardiac -Blue)
Boils (also Orange)
Canker Sores
Chronic Diseases
Cholera (Blue)
Congestions (Scarlet)
Croup
Dysentery (Blue)
Erysipelas
Exhaustion
Germs
Gum Boils
Headaches (Turquoise, Indigo, Blue, Violet)
Heart (Yellow, Violet)
Hepatitis
Infertility
Influenza
Insomnia (Violet, Green)
Jaundice
Kidneys (Orange, Scarlet, Indigo, Violet)
Liver (Scarlet, Yellow, Violet, Upper Lobes- Blue)
Lumbar Region of Spine (Indigo)
Mucous (Red, Lemon)
Neuralgia (Red, Violet)
Parathyroid
Pituitary Diseases
Shell Shock
Skin (Scarlet)
Stomach (Scarlet, Blue, Indigo, Violet, Troubles – Yellow)
Syphilis (Blue)
Throat (Blue)
Thyroid
Ulcers (Yellow)

Vaso-motor System (Indigo)
Virus
Whooping Cough (Indigo)

Turquoise

Fatigue Poisons
Fevers (Blue, Violet)
Headaches (Indigo, Blue, Violet, Green)
Hot Liquid Burns
Infections
Pressure, Swelling of the Head
Skin Injuries, leaves no scars
Sunburn

Blue

Apoplexy
Adrenal Function
Bleeding Piles
High Blood Pressure/Hypertension, Cardiac (also Violet, Green)
Bowels (also Indigo)
Bruises
Bubonic Plague
Burns
Carcinoma
Chapped Hands
Chicken Pox
Cholera (Green)
Cholic
Cuts
Dandruff (Violet)
Diaphragm
Diarrhea (Indigo)
Dysentery (Green)
Ears (Indigo, Yellow)
Cancer, Epithelial
Eruptions
Esophagus
Femur (Violet)
Fevers (Turquoise, Violet)

Gastritis
Goiter
Gonorrhea
Headaches (Turquoise, Indigo, Violet, Green)
Hemorrhages
High Temperature (Violet)
Hot Blood
Hoarseness
Hydrophobia Bite
Iliac Arteries
Ilium
Inflamed Eyes
Inflamed Gums
Inflammatory Pain
Insomnia (Violet, Green)
Invalidism
Jaws
Larynx
Liver, Upper Lobe (Scarlet, Yellow, Green, Violet)
Lung Hemorrhage
Lungs, Upper Lobe
Loss of Voice, due to Shock – Along with Violet
Mammary Glands (Violet)
Measles (Red)
Menstrual Pains (Scarlet)
Neck
Palate
Painful Stomach
Purging
Rectal Troubles (Rectum Ulcers – Violet)
Rheumatic Conditions, Acute (Chronic - Orange, Yellow)
Scarlet Fever (Orange, Red)
Sacral Region of the Spine
Sciatic Nerve Troubles (Violet)
Sore Mouth
Stomach (Scarlet, Green, Indigo, Violet, Troubles – Yellow)
Syphilis (Green)

Stings
Teething
Thighs (Violet)
Throat (Green)
Toothache, inflamed teeth (Violet)
Tonsils
Tumors (Violet)
Veins
Vomiting
Womb Troubles

Indigo

Asthma (chronic, use orange)
Blindness
Bloodshot Eyes
Bowels (also Blue)
Breast
Bronchial Croup
Bronchitis (Orange, Red, Yellow)
Cataract
Colds (Lemon, Green, Orange, Red)
Convulsions
Consumption (Red)
Cranium
Creeping Palsy
Deafness
Delirium
Diarrhea (Blue)
Diuresis
Dyspepsia (Yellow)
Earache
Ears (Blue, Yellow)
Emesis
Excretory System
Pain, Extreme & Acute
Eyes (Yellow)
Facial Paralysis
Granular (Inflamed) Eyes
Gout (Orange)
Headaches (Turquoise, Blue, Violet, Green)
Inflammations
Kidneys (Orange, Scarlet, Green, Violet)
Knees
Lungs (Violet, Yellow, Upper Lobe- Blue)
Lumbar Region of Spine (Green)
Nose
Nose Bleeds

Overheating
Overactive Thyroid
Phthisis (Tuberculosis)
Pneumonia (Red)
Pulmonary Diseases (Violet)
Sacral Plexus
Skeleton
Skin Eruptions
Smelling Difficulties
Spasms
Stomach (Scarlet, Green, Blue, Violet, Troubles – Yellow)
Styes
Sweat Glands
Swellings
Tissue Degeneration
Trouble Breathing
Ulcerated Cornea
Vaso-motor System (Green)
Weak bones (Lemon)
Whooping Cough (Green)

Violet

Ankles
Bacteria (with infection use Ruby)
Baldness
Bladder Trouble
Calves
Cerebro-Spinal Meningitis
Poor Circulation (Red)
Concussion
Congestion of Nerves
Cramps
Dandruff (Blue)
Dormant Stomach
Epigastric Ganglion
Epilepsy (Orange)
Feet
Femur (Blue)
Fevers (Turquoise, Blue)
Headaches (Turquoise, Indigo, Blue, Green)
Heart (Yellow, Green)
High Blood Pressure/Hypertension (also green, cardiac - blue)
High Temperature (Blue)
Hips
Impure Blood
Insomnia (Blue, Green)
Kidneys (Orange, Scarlet, Green, Indigo, Violet)
Leucorrhea
Liver (Scarlet, Yellow, Green, Upper Lobes- Blue)
Lungs (Indigo, Yellow, Upper Lobe- Blue)
Loss of Voice, due to Shock – Along with Blue
Low White Blood Corpuscle Count (Yellow)
Lymphatic Ailments (Yellow)
Malaria
Mammary Glands (Blue)
Nasal Catarrh
Neisserian Infections/Gonorrhea

Neuralgia (Green, Red)
Over-Active Kidneys
Parasites (Ruby)
Pulmonary Diseases (Indigo)
Rectum, Ulcers (Rectal Troubles, Blue)
Ringworm
Scalp Diseases
Sciatic Nerve Troubles (Blue)
Spleen
Stomach (Scarlet, Green, Blue, Indigo, Violet, Troubles – Yellow)
Sympathetic Nervous System
Thighs (Blue)
Toes
Toothache (Blue - inflamed teeth)
Toxemia
Tuberculosis (Red, Ruby, Yellow)
Tumors (Blue)
Ulcerated Uterus

GLOSSARY OF TERMS

Alimentary Tract Energizer - activates the food passages.

Alterative - produces a favorable change in the process of nutrition and repair in recent disorders.

Analgesic - decreases sensitivity to pain.

Anaphrodisiac - decreases sexual desires.

Anesthesia - puts one to sleep and deadens pain.

Anodyne - soothes suffering.

Antacid - neutralizes or counteracts acidity.

Anthelmintic - destructive to worms.

Antiarchitic - corrects Rickets, bone softness and soft teeth.

Anti-Inflammatory - decreases burning and inflammation.

Anti-Malarial - prevents or removes Malaria.

Antipruritic - prevents or relieves itching.

Antipyretic - lowers the body temperature.

Antiseptic - prevents decay.

Antiscorbutic - corrects scurvy, a disorder of nutrition and dietetic errors.

Anti-spasmodic - removes, prevents, or decreases spasms.

Aphrodisiac - sex builder, arouses sexual desires and builds the sex powers by enhancing sensitivity.

Arterial Depressant - lowers the blood pressure to give relief from many headaches and pressure pains.

Aromatic - induces the qualities of Spices, changes the odor and smell.

Astringent - causes contraction and arrests discharges.

Auric Builder - guilds the aura or electro-magnetic field of the chemical body.

Bactericide - destroys bacteria and micro-organisms.

Cardiac Depressant - relaxes and soothes the muscles and nerves controlling the heart.

Carminative - relieves flatulence or distension of the stomach and intestines with gases. Relieves cramps throughout the digestive system.

Caustic - burns or corrodes.

Cathartic - produces increased bowel action.

Cerebral Depressant - decreases the functional activity of the brain.

Cholagogue - accelerates the flow of Bile.

Counter-Irritant - allays irritation.

Demulcent - allays irritation of abraded and scratched surfaces.

Detergent - cleans.

Diaphoretic - increases the perspiration.

Digestant - aids the process of converting food into materials fit to be absorbed and assimilated into the physical body, by stimulating the gastric and intestinal glands and pancreas.

Disinfectant - destroys rotting materials.

Diuretic - increases or promotes the secretion of front elimination.

Emetic - induces vomiting by irritation.

Emmenagogue - stimulates the ovarian elimination or menstruation.

Emotional Stabilizer - stabilizes the emotions.

Exobolic - causes or accelerates expulsion of a fetus or unborn baby.

Expectorant - promotes the ejection by spitting of mucous or other fluids from the lungs or windpipe.

Febrifuge - dispels or reduces fevers.

Genital Excitant - stirs the functional activity of the generative organs.

Galactogogue - increases the secretion of milk after childbirth, by stimulating the mammary glands, to aid in supplying milk for the baby. This eliminates the need to use artificial formulas made from cow's or goat's milk. Mother's milk is nature's best natural feeding for a baby, especially if she eats the best of foods.

Germicide - destroys germs and bacteria.

Hemoglobin Builder - builds the coloring matter of the red blood corpuscles in the liver.

Hemostatic - checks the flow of blood.

Hypnotic - induces sleep.

Inspissator - dries or thickens.

Irritant - irritates.

Laxative - mildly loosens the intestines and moves the bowels.

Leukocyte Builder - builds the white corpuscles in the spleen.

Liver Energizer - activates the liver.

Lung Builder - builds and stimulates the lungs (used for Tuberculosis).

Lymphatic Depressant - decreases the functional activity of the lymphatic glands for nutrition, and helps the appetite in reducing overweight conditions.

Motor Stimulant - increases the functional activity of the motor nervous system which energizes the muscles into action.

Narcotic - produces stupor.

Nerve Builder - builds the nerves by stimulating the Choroid Gland for cerebrospinal fluid secretion.

Pain Reliever - allays suffering.

Parathyroid Stimulant - increases the functional activity of the four parathyroid glands, embedded in the right and left Thyroid Glands.

Phagocyte Builder - builds the cells which destroy harmful micro-organisms.

Pituitary Stimulant - increases the functional activity of the Pituitary Gland.

Purificatory - purifies.

Pustulant - suppurates.

Renal Energizer - increases the function and activity of the Kidneys.

Respiratory Depressant - decreases breathing.

Rubefacient - reddens the skin.

Sedative - allays activity and excitement; causing sleep.

Sensory Stimulant - increases the activity of the sensory nervous system, energizing the sight, smell, touch, taste and hearing.

Splenic Depressant - decreases the functional activity of the spleen.

Splenic Stimulant - increases the functional activity of the spleen.

Stomachic - tones the stomach.

Suprarenal Stimulant – increases the functional action of the adrenal glands on the kidney.

Thymus Activator - increases the action of the Thymus Gland.

Thyroid Depressant - decreases the functional Thyroid Gland.

Tonic - tones the whole system.

Vasoconstrictor — causes contraction of the blood vessels, raising the blood pressure.

Vasodilator - causes expansion of the blood vessels, lowering the blood pressure.

Vesicant - blisters.

Vitality Builder - builds the life principle by stimulating the Pineal Gland.